PENNSYLVANIA DUTCH COUNTRY

ANNA DUBROVSKY

Contents

Pennsylvania Dutch Country

Look for ★ to find recommended
sights, activities, dining, and lodging.

Highlights

★ **Amish Attractions:** If you learned every-thing you know about the Amish from the movie *Witness*, you've got a lot to learn. Get schooled at Plain & Fancy Farm, the Amish Farm and House, or the Mennonite Information Center (page 11).

★ **Strasburg Rail Road:** Take a trip to Paradise on the nation's oldest operating short-line railroad (page 18).

★ **Air Museums:** Take to the skies in an antique plane, or take a trip back in time during World War II Weekend (page 41).

★ **Hawk Mountain Sanctuary:** Some 20,000 hawks, eagles, and falcons soar past this rap-tor sanctuary on their southward journey. The sight is awe-inspiring and the hiking terrific (page 43).

★ **The Hershey Story:** One of Pennsylvania's newest museums, The Hershey Story offers hands-on experience in chocolate-making (page 51).

★ **Hersheypark:** Hershey's century-old amusement park has been adding coasters like they're going out of style (page 53).

★ **Gettysburg National Military Park:** Site of the Civil War's most hellish battle, this national park is heaven for history buffs (page 82).

S outh-central Pennsylvania has no blockbuster cities. Its largest, Reading, has fewer than 90,000 residents. And yet, tourism is a multibillion-dollar industry here. Part of the reason is the public's fascination with the Amish, whose way of life is in sharp contrast to the average American's. Lancaster County, the most popular destination in Dutch country, boasts the largest concentration of Amish in the world. Their use of horse-drawn buggies, adherence to strict dress codes, and rejection of technologies including television and computers makes them exotic. A casual drive through Lancaster County's fertile farmlands has a safari-esque quality. ("Look, honey, buggy at three o'clock!") Unlike giraffes and elephants, the Amish take offense to being photographed, so resist the temptation to aim your camera at the farmer working his fields with mule-drawn equipment, the children driving a pony cart, or the women selling their pies and preserves at a market stand.

There's more to the region's allure than the Amish experience. Less than 40 miles from the heart of Amish country is the town of Hershey, the product of one chocolatier's expansive vision. Few places offer as high a concentration of family-friendly attractions as "The Sweetest Place on Earth." In the southern part of Pennsylvania Dutch country is the town of Gettysburg, site of the Civil War's bloodiest battle and President Abraham Lincoln's most memorable speech. The place throbs with history—and not just on days when it's awash with musket-toting reenactors. The region is also home to the state capital, Harrisburg, and York County, the self-proclaimed "Factory Tour Capital of the World."

Travelers unfamiliar with the term *Pennsylvania Dutch* may wonder what south-central Pennsylvania has to do with the Netherlands. The answer is: nada. "Dutch," in this case, is generally regarded as a corruption of the word *Deutsch,* the German word for "German." Tens of thousands of German-speaking Europeans immigrated to Pennsylvania in the 18th century (before Germany as we know it existed). They, their descendants, and their English-influenced

---

Previous: Gettysburg; Amish buggy; Countries of Origin Chocolate Tasting at The Hershey Story. **Above:** the dome of the State Capitol.

Pennsylvania Dutch Country

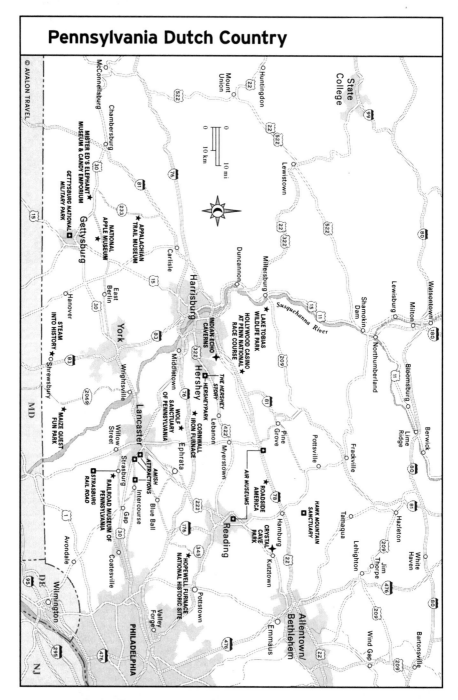

dialect came to be called Pennsylvania German, or Pennsylvania Dutch. A common misconception is that "Pennsylvania Dutch" is synonymous with "Amish." In fact, the Amish made up a very small percentage of the Germanic settlers. The overwhelming majority were affiliated with Lutheran or Reformed churches. But the Amish and a handful of related "plain" groups have emerged as the guardians of the Pennsylvania Dutch dialect. They speak it at home and among friends. Amish children learn English as part of their formal education, which typically takes place in a one-room schoolhouse (think *Little House on the Prairie*) and ends after the eighth grade. *Wilkom* to Pennsylvania Dutch country.

PLANNING YOUR TIME

You could spend weeks exploring the small, smaller, and smallest towns of Pennsylvania Dutch country, but three or four days is sufficient time to hit the highlights. Plan to spend at least a day tootling around Lancaster County's Amish countryside, sharing the roads with horse-drawn buggies and buying direct from farmers and bakers, quilters and furniture makers. Keep in mind that the Amish and their "plain" cousins don't do business on Sundays. See to it that you eat at a restaurant serving Pennsylvania Dutch fare, preferably one that offers family-style dining. If your agenda also includes outlet shopping, save it for the evening. The Rockvale and Tanger outlets, just minutes apart along Lancaster County's main east-west thoroughfare, are open until 9pm every day but Sunday. Anyone into antiques should plan to spend Sunday in Adamstown, aka "Antiques Capital USA," about 20 miles northeast of Lancaster city.

The Lancaster area is a good base of operations for exploring other parts of Pennsylvania Dutch country. Reading is about 30 miles to Lancaster's northeast, Hershey and Harrisburg are 30-40 miles to its northwest, and Gettysburg is 55 miles to its southwest. There was a time when demand for rooms in Lancaster County far exceeded supply. Some visitors slept in their cars; others settled for hotels and motels as far as an hour away. The local chamber of commerce beseeched residents with spare rooms to open their doors to Amish-obsessed tourists, and many answered the call. Today the county boasts more than 150 B&Bs.

If you have kids, a visit to Hershey is non-negotiable. You'll run yourself ragged trying to hit all the attractions in one day, so set aside two. A day is generally enough for Gettysburg, but ardent history buffs and ghost hunters can keep busy for several.

Your trip through rural Lancaster County may take you over a covered bridge.

Lancaster County

In January 1955, *Plain and Fancy* opened on Broadway. The musical comedy is the story of two New Yorkers who travel to Bird-in-Hand, Pennsylvania—a real-life village amid Lancaster County's Amish farmlands—to sell a piece of property they've inherited. There, just a few hours from home, they encounter a way of life completely foreign to them. The Amish, or "plain," lifestyle was completely foreign to most playgoers, too. A modest success on Broadway, the show sparked enormous interest in its setting. Before *Plain and Fancy,* Lancaster County was lucky to get 25,000 visitors a year. After, the number rocketed to more than two million. Tourists traipsed through farm fields, knocked on doors, and peered through windows in their quest for a close encounter of the Amish kind. Today there's no need to trespass. Lancaster County, which now welcomes upwards of 10 million visitors annually, is flush with information centers, attractions, and tour operators offering an Amish 101 curriculum.

About 282,000 Amish live in North America, according to the Young Center for Anabaptist and Pietist Studies at Lancaster County's Elizabethtown College. Though the church originated in Europe, it's extinct there. Lancaster County is home to about 33,000 Amish—roughly half of Pennsylvania's Amish—and is neck and neck with Ohio's Holmes County for the distinction of having the world's largest Amish settlement. It also holds the distinction of having the oldest surviving Amish settlement in the world. The first ship carrying a significant group of Amish from their homelands in central Europe to the New World docked in Philadelphia in 1737. Some of the Amish passengers made their home in Lancaster County; a larger number settled 20-odd miles away in present-day Berks County. While the Amish all but disappeared from Berks County by the early 1800s, Lancaster County had six congregations (known as church districts) at the close of the century. Their numbers have soared since then, more than doubling between 1980 and 2000 and climbing more than 30 percent in the first decade of this century. Large families have

Bird-in-Hand

Lancaster County

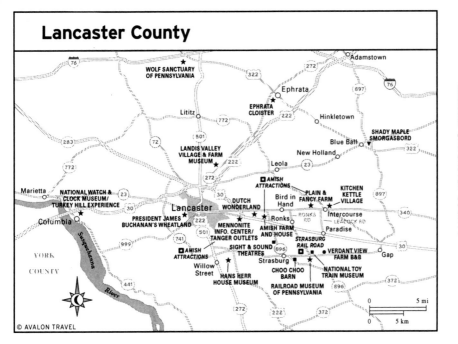

a lot to do with the vigorous growth: most Amish couples have five or more children. And while many Amish teens are allowed a period of *rumspringa,* or "running around," during which they decide whether to join the church, very few leave the fold. Given the chance to drive cars and dress how they please, about 85 percent ultimately choose the horse and buggy as their mode of transport and the distinctive garb that sets them apart from the "English," i.e., everyone else.

As you explore the region, keep in mind that not all traditionally dressed people are Amish. Some conservative Mennonite and Brethren groups also practice "plain" dress. You may not be able to tell them apart, but each has distinguishing characteristics.

There's more to Lancaster County than its Amish population. The county seat, Lancaster city, boasts a thriving arts scene. Rail fans will find an abundance of train-related attractions in and around the town of Strasburg. Antiques enthusiasts will fall in love with Adamstown, aka "Antiques Capital USA." Bargain hunters

can get their fix at a pair of outlet malls along Route 30. Anyone fascinated by the Amish and their strict codes of conduct will likely be fascinated by the towns of Lititz and Ephrata. The former began as an experiment in utopia by members of a Protestant denomination that prohibited everything from dancing to changing professions without approval from church elders. The latter was home to a religious group so disdainful of worldly pleasures that its members slept on wooden pillows. Other Lancaster County communities are remarkable for their names: Intercourse, Paradise, Blue Ball, Fertility, and, of course, Bird-in-Hand.

★ AMISH ATTRACTIONS

If you're visiting Lancaster County for the number one reason people visit Lancaster County—to see the Amish—you may be at a loss as to where to start. Unlike malls and museums, amusement parks and ski resorts, the Amish are an attraction without an address. You can't punch "Amish" into your GPS and get turn-by-turn directions. They're people living their lives—people who don't necessarily appreciate being the focus of tourists' attention. And while it's not hard to catch sight of them living their lives, you'll shortchange yourself if you don't garner some understanding of why they live the way they do.

Plain & Fancy Farm, the Amish Farm and House, and the Mennonite Information Center are great places to acquaint yourself with the ways of the Amish. Visiting one is quite enough. Each offers a hearty menu of get-to-know-the-Amish options. Choosing between the attractions is a matter of taste. Plain & Fancy is smack-dab in the heart of Amish country, while the other two are located along Route 30, a major east-west thoroughfare. It's the only one that offers buggy rides through Amish countryside and the opportunity to visit an Amish family in their home, but it's also the priciest of the three. The Amish Farm and House is your best bet if you're traveling with kids. It's crawling with animals and offers a variety of children's activities, including pony rides, a corn maze, and "Buttercup," a life-size fiberglass cow always ready to be milked. While all three offer driving tours of the countryside, the Mennonite Information Center is unique in that it doesn't

operate tour buses. Instead, a guide will climb into your car and lead you on a personal tour. It's the way to go if you tend to ask loads of questions. It's also a great value: just $49 for a vehicle carrying as many as seven people. On the downside, the Mennonite Information Center is closed on Sundays.

Plain & Fancy Farm

In 1958, a few years after *Plain and Fancy* hit the Broadway stage, a man named Walter Smith built an Amish-style house and barn along Route 340, midway between the villages of Bird-in-Hand and Intercourse, with the intent of giving house tours and holding barn dances. Shrewdly, he named the property after the Broadway musical that ignited so much interest in Amish country. Half a century later, **Plain & Fancy Farm** (3121 Old Philadelphia Pike, Bird-in-Hand, www.plainandfancyfarm.com) offers everything a tourist could want: food, lodging, souvenirs, and an excellent orientation to the Amish way of life.

A good place to begin your orientation: the **Amish Experience Theater** (717/768-8400, ext. 210, www.amishexperience.com, open daily mid-Mar.-Nov. and select days in Dec., shows on the hour 10am-5pm, admission $10.95, children 4-12 $7.95). This is not

a one-room schoolhouse at the Amish Farm and House

your garden-variety movie theater. Designed to look like a barn, it features five screens, a fog machine, and other bells and whistles that produce three-dimensional effects. *Jacob's Choice,* the film for which the theater was built, packs some 400 years of history into 40 minutes. It's the contemporary story of an Old Order Amish family and the teenage son torn between joining the church and leaving the fold for a modern life. As the title character learns about the persecution his religious ancestors faced in Europe and their journey to the New World, so does the audience. Filmed locally in 1995, *Jacob's Choice* doesn't dwell on the blood and gore, but a burning-at-the-stake scene could rattle children.

The Amish-style house Mr. Smith built back in 1958 is still open for tours. Tickets can be purchased at the Amish Experience Theater box office. Now known as the **Amish Country Homestead** (open daily mid-Mar.-late Nov. and select days in Dec., admission $10.95, children 4-12 $7.95), the nine-room house is continually updated to reflect changes in the Amish lifestyle. (Contrary to popular belief, the Amish don't live just as they did centuries ago.) Guides explain such head-scratchers as why the Amish eschew electricity but use refrigerators and other appliances powered by propane gas. The tour takes about 45 minutes. Combo tickets for the theater and house tour are available.

Several minibus tours depart from the theater. The most popular is the **Amish Farmlands Tour** (daily mid-Mar.-Nov. and select days in Dec., $27.95, children 12 and under $15.95), a 90-minute cruise through the surrounding countryside. Guides are well-versed in the Amish way of life. A "SuperSaver Package" is available for those who wish to experience *Jacob's Choice,* the house tour, and the Farmlands Tour.

Other tours include the **Visit-in-Person Tour** (June-Nov., $49.95), which gives visitors the opportunity to interact with Amish locals. Participants visit an Amish dairy farm during milking time and then an Amish craftsperson. The three-hour excursion culminates in a sit-down chat at an Amish home. It often sells out, so it's a good idea to purchase tickets in advance. Harrison Ford fans may opt for the **Witness Tour** (May-Oct., $49.95), featuring a visit to the farm where he filmed the 1985 thriller *Witness.*

The bus tours are top-notch, but if you're short on time or traveling with kids, a buggy ride is the way to go. **Aaron and Jessica's Buggy Rides** (9am-dusk Mon.-Sat. and 10am-5pm Sun. Apr.-Nov., 9am-4:30pm Mon.-Sat. Dec.-Mar., 717/768-8828, www.amishbuggyrides.com) depart from Plain & Fancy Farm on a regular basis. Trips range from 20 minutes to more than an hour, with prices starting at $10 for adults and $5 for children 3-12. Aaron and Jessica's—named for owner Jack Meyer's oldest daughter and her first horse—bills itself as Lancaster County's only buggy tour operator staffed entirely by "plain" people (except on Sundays, which they set aside for worship).

Plain & Fancy Farm's main attraction is its restaurant, famous for its family-style meals. The on-site AmishView Inn & Suites makes Plain & Fancy Farm a 24-hour attraction.

The Amish Farm and House

The easiest way to find the **Amish Farm and House** (2395 Lincoln Hwy. East, Lancaster, 717/394-6185, www.amishfarmandhouse. com, 10am-4pm daily Jan.-Mar., 9am-5pm daily Apr.-May, 9am-6pm daily June-Aug., 9am-5pm daily Sept.-Oct., 10am-4pm daily Nov.-Dec., admission $8.95, seniors $7.95, children 5-11 $5.95) is to look for its neighbor, a Target. The store opened in 2005 on property carved from the hundreds-year-old farm, and its bull's-eye logo is easier to spot than the barn, silo, and windmill that once dominated the skyline. Their juxtaposition is emblematic of the Amish community's insoluble dilemma: modernity.

Opened to the public in July 1955, the Amish Farm and House bills itself as the first tourist attraction in Lancaster County and the first Amish attraction in the United States. The operating farm has since shrunk from 25 acres to 15 (making room for Target, PetSmart, Panera, etc.), but there's more to see than ever. Start with a guided tour of the farmhouse, included in general admission. Built in 1805 of limestone quarried on the property, the house has counted Quakers, Mennonites, and Amish as residents. Today it's furnished in the manner of a typical Amish home. The front room features wooden benches arranged in preparation for a church service, opening the door for a discussion of why the Amish worship in their homes and other aspects of their religion. Their manner of dress is explained in the bedrooms. After the 45-minute tour, explore the farm at your own pace. Children love the chicken house and the 1803 barn with its cows, horses, and pigs. A goat playground makes for great photo ops with the frisky ruminants. Kids (we're talking humans now, not goats) also enjoy the corn maze, up and running mid-July through October, and tootling around on Amish scooters when weather permits. The farm also has an original tobacco shed, one of the few remaining lime kilns in Lancaster County, a working waterwheel, a circa 1855 covered bridge, and a one-room Amish schoolhouse built specifically for tourists in 2006.

The Amish Farm and House offers 90-minute **Countryside Tours** ($19.95, children 5-11 $12.95, children 4 and under $4.95) year-round. Reservations are recommended, especially in the warmer months. The mini-bus tours usually stop at an Amish roadside stand or two (except on Sundays, when the Amish don't conduct business). Combo tickets for the house, farm, and bus tour are available.

Mennonite Information Center

Don't be put off by its name. You *will* learn about the Amish at the **Mennonite Information Center** (2209 Millstream Rd., Lancaster, 717/299-0954, www.mennoniteinfoctr.com, 8am-5pm Mon.-Sat. Apr.-Oct., 8:30am-4:30pm Mon.-Sat. Nov.-Mar.), located next to Tanger Outlets. Start by watching the three-screen feature *Who Are the Amish?* (on the hour 9am-4pm, $6, children 6-16 $4). It answers such questions as: How many are there? Why do they dress that way? Why do they drive buggies? And what do they have against electricity? The images are beautiful and the narration intelligent, but at 30 minutes long, the movie won't necessarily hold the attention of young children. Also showing: *Postcards From a Heritage of Faith,* which elucidates the similarities and differences between the Amish and

A buggy ride is a great way to see the countryside.

Mennonites, both of whom trace their roots to the Anabaptist movement in 16th-century Europe. (Anabaptists rejected infant baptism and advocated for separation of church and state, for which they faced severe persecution.) There's no charge to see the 17-minute film, shown on the half hour. Admission to the center's exhibits on Anabaptist life is also free.

Movies and exhibits are nice, but what sets the Mennonite Information Center apart are its **personal tours of Amish country.** For about the cost of two seats on other countryside tours, a guide will hop in your vehicle and point the way to Amish farms, one-room schoolhouses, quilt shops, covered bridges, etc. All guides have a Mennonite or Amish heritage. The rate for a vehicle with 1-7 people is $49 for two hours, $16 for each additional hour. Call ahead to arrange for a tour at a specified time or just show up and request one. The wait for a guide is rarely longer than 30 minutes. Another great service from the Mennonite Information Center is its list of **Mennonite guest homes,** available on its website and in pamphlet form at the center.

The center is home to a life-size reproduction of the portable place of worship described in the biblical book of Exodus. A wax figure of the high priest sports a breastplate of gold and precious stones. The **Biblical Tabernacle Reproduction** (admission $7.50, children 6-16 $5) can only be seen by guided tour, offered at regular intervals year-round. The reproduction has no real connection to Lancaster County's Anabaptist communities. It was constructed in the 1940s by a Baptist minister in St. Petersburg, Florida, purchased by Mennonites in the 1950s, and installed in its current home in the 1970s.

The information center sells a variety of tabernacle model kits, fair-trade handicrafts from around the world, and a wide selection of books about Anabaptist history and faith.

Next door to the center is the headquarters of the **Lancaster Mennonite Historical Society** (2215 Millstream Rd., 717/393-9745, www.lmhs.org, 8:30am-4:30pm Tues.-Sat.), which also boasts a fantastic bookstore. It

has a museum (admission $5, seniors $4.50, students $3) that showcases Pennsylvania German artifacts.

DOWNTOWN LANCASTER

It's not unusual for tourists to come and go from Lancaster County without stepping foot in downtown Lancaster. Many are entirely unaware that the county has an urban center. It's hard to blame them. Lancaster County's countryside and quaint towns have gotten all the press for decades. It doesn't help that its major east-west thoroughfare, Route 30, bypasses downtown Lancaster altogether. Well, downtown's museums and merchants have had just about enough of being ignored. Revitalization efforts in recent years have given downtown a fresh look and its boosters more cred. Now, in addition to boasting the oldest continuously operated farmers market and theater in the United States, downtown boasts a new convention center and adjoining 19-floor hotel. New restaurants, stores, and galleries add to its promotional arsenal. Plan on devoting a day to downtown. Make it a Tuesday, Friday, or Saturday, when the farmers market is open. Ideally, make it the first or third Friday of any given month, when many galleries, boutiques, and other businesses extend their hours. **First Fridays** (5pm-9pm, 717/291-4758, www.lancasterarts.com) feature special exhibitions, artist receptions, and other arts-related events. Live music wafts from one doorway after another on third Fridays, known as **Music Fridays** (717/291-4758, www.lancastercityevents.com).

Walking Tour

The city of Lancaster is so steeped in history—it was capital of the 13 colonies for one day during the American Revolution and capital of Pennsylvania for 13 years—that a guided tour is a good idea. Led by a volunteer guide in 18th- or 19th-century garb, the **Historic Lancaster Walking Tour** (Lancaster Visitors Center, 5 W. King St., 717/392-1776, www.historiclancasterwalkingtour.com, $7, seniors $6, college students $4, children 6-18 $1) visits dozens of sites. Allow about 90 minutes for the tour, which begins with a DVD presentation. It's offered at 1pm daily April-October. On Tuesdays, Fridays, and Saturdays, when nearby Central Market is open, tours depart at 10am as well as 1pm.

Central Market

Central Market (23 N. Market St., 717/735-6890, www.centralmarketlancaster.com, 6am-4pm Tues. and Fri., 6am-2pm Sat.) is the pulsing heart of the city. Granted, the indoor farmers market pulses just three days a week, but given its advanced age, it's incredible that it pulses at all. Central Market is the oldest continually operated farmers market in the country. When Lancaster was laid out in the 1730s, a lot adjacent to the town square was designated as a public marketplace in perpetuity. In its early years, the market was simply an open space where farmers and others could sell their wares. The current market house, an eye-catching Romanesque Revival structure with two towers and ornate brick and stone work, was built in 1889. Many of the 60-some market stalls have been operated by multiple generations of the same family. The Stoner's vegetable stall, famous for its arugula, has been around for more than a century. Fresh produce isn't the half of it. Central Market is one-stop shopping for everything from hand-stitched Amish quilts to foie gras. There's beef, poultry, and fish; milk and cheeses; breads and pastries; coffees and teas; candies and candles; preserves and prepared foods. There's even a stall devoted to horseradish. Come on the early side for the best selection. On Tuesdays and Fridays, some vendors call it quits at 3pm, an hour before the market closes.

Art Museums and Galleries

Lancaster has a thriving arts scene, with several dozen galleries, artist studios, fine craft stores, and art museums. It has an art college and even an art-themed hotel. The **Lancaster City Arts** (717/291-4758, www.lancasterarts. com) website is a good resource for visitors who wish to explore the scene. There's no better place to start than **Gallery Row,** roughly defined as the section of Prince Street between Walnut Street and King Street to its south. Notable tenants include the **Red Raven Art Company** (138 N. Prince St., 717/299-4400, www.redravenartcompany.com, 10am-5pm Tues. and Thurs.-Sat., open until 8:30pm First Fridays), which showcases a diverse array of fine art. If you're partial to folk art, you'll dig **CityFolk** (146 N. Prince St., 717/393-8807,

a bird's-eye view of downtown Lancaster

www.cityfolkonprince.com, 10am-4pm Tues.-Sat., open until 9pm First Fridays) with its ever-changing galleries of furniture, paintings, carvings, pottery, and other works.

A couple of blocks east of Gallery Row is the onetime home of Lancaster's most acclaimed artist, the Modernist painter Charles Demuth. It's now open to the public as the **Demuth Museum** (120 E. King St., 717/299-9940, www.demuth.org, 10am-4pm Tues.-Sat., 1pm-4pm Sun., closed Jan., free admission). Demuth was born in Lancaster in 1883 and died there in 1935 but moved in avant-garde circles in places as far-flung as Paris, New York, and Bermuda. He was very much appreciated during his lifetime, earning a place in the permanent collection of New York's Metropolitan Museum of Art by his 40s. Rotating exhibits showcase works by Demuth's contemporaries or artists with a thematic or stylistic connection to him.

Not to be forgotten is the **Lancaster Museum of Art** (135 N. Lime St., 717/394-3497, www.lmapa.org, 10am-4pm Tues.-Sat., noon-4pm Sun., free admission), home to an extensive collection of works by contemporary regional artists. The museum building is a remarkably intact example of Greek Revival-style domestic architecture. The Grubb Mansion, as it's called, was built in the 1840s for an iron master with an eye for art.

Lancaster Science Factory

Geared toward children 7-13, the **Lancaster Science Factory** (454 New Holland Ave., 717/509-6363, www.lancastersciencefactory.org, 10am-5pm Tues.-Sat., noon-5pm Sun., open Mon. Memorial Day-Labor Day, admission $8, seniors $7, children 3-15 $6.50) features dozens of interactive exhibits that help visitors—even those well over 13—understand such things as electricity, magnetism, acoustics, and fluid dynamics. If your kids like blowing bubbles, they'll love the *Minimal Surfaces* exhibit. Budding Beethovens can experiment with the "bongophone," a bongo/xylophone. The Fac, which opened in 2008 after five years in the making, isn't the only

science museum in Lancaster. Less than two miles away is the **North Museum of Natural History & Science** (400 College Ave., 717/291-3941, www.northmuseum.org, 10am-5pm Tues.-Sat., noon-5pm Sun., admission $7.50, seniors and children 3-17 $6.50, museum and planetarium admission $10, seniors and children $9), which boasts a dinosaur gallery, live animal room, and planetarium.

"TRAIN TOWN USA"

The town of **Strasburg,** some nine miles southwest of downtown Lancaster, bills itself as "the real Lancaster County." Which is to say that it has changed little in the last couple of centuries. Buggies clip-clop through the town square at the intersection of Routes 741 and 896. Families stream in and out of the old-timey **Strasburg Country Store & Creamery** (1 W. Main St., Strasburg, 717/687-0766, www.strasburg.com, open daily), where scoops of homemade ice cream are pressed into just-made waffle cones. Much of *Witness*, the 1985 romantic thriller that did more for tourism to Amish country than any marketing campaign, was filmed on a farm nearby.

But what brings tourists here by the busload is train mania. There are half a dozen train-related attractions within two miles of the square, including the **Red Caboose Motel and Restaurant** (312 Paradise Ln., Ronks, 717/687-5000, www.redcaboosemotel.com, accommodations $70-160, food $4-17), where rail fans bed down and chow down in refurbished train cars and cabooses. The Strasburg area is such a magnet for "foamers," as the most zealous of rail fans are known, that it's sometimes called "Train Town USA" (not to be confused with "Railroad City," aka Altoona, three hours away). The oldest of the attractions and a good place to start is the Strasburg Rail Road. Don't leave town without a visit to the Choo Choo Barn, where you can see the historic railroad and much more in miniature.

From the town square, head east on Route 741 (Main Street). You'll see the Choo Choo Barn on your right after half a mile. Half a mile later, you'll arrive at the Strasburg Rail Road and Railroad Museum of Pennsylvania, located on opposite sides of Route 741. Continue to the next intersection and turn left onto Paradise Lane to check into the Red Caboose or check out the National Toy Train Museum.

★ Strasburg Rail Road

Incorporated in 1832, the **Strasburg Rail Road** (300 Gap Rd., Ronks, 866/725-9666, www.strasburgrailroad.com) is America's oldest operating short-line railroad. It was almost abandoned in the late 1950s, after an upsurge in the use of highways for freight transportation and a series of storms that destroyed parts of its 4.5-mile track. But rail fans came to its rescue, turning it into a tourist attraction and time capsule of early-1900s railroading. The Strasburg Rail Road offers trips to Paradise and back—as in Paradise, Pennsylvania—every month but January. Steam locomotives pull painstakingly restored passenger cars past farm fields plowed by horses and mules. Amish buggies wait at railroad crossings.

Ticket prices vary widely, depending on the type of excursion and your choice of passenger car. In addition to standard rides, which depart hourly on most operating days, the Strasburg Rail Road offers a wide variety of themed trips, from murder mystery dinners to "The Great Train Robbery" to "Santa's Paradise Express." On select days each June, September, and November, fans of Thomas the Tank Engine can ride behind a steam locomotive based on the storybook character. **"Day Out With Thomas"** and other themed trips sometimes sell out, so it's a good idea to purchase tickets in advance.

The round-trip takes just 45 minutes, but train buffs and families with young children should plan to spend a couple of hours at the home station. A guided tour of the railroad's mechanical shop ($18) is offered at noon on most operating days. It's limited to 25 people and often sells out. Kids can operate a vintage pump car along a short track or ride in a circa 1920 miniature steam train. A train-themed play area was added in 2013. The station also features gift shops geared toward train lovers, a toy store with a large selection of Thomas the Tank Engine merchandise, and a café. Consider packing a picnic basket or buying a box lunch at the station and disembarking the train at one of two picnic groves. Groff's Grove is popular with families because it has vintage playground equipment and is convenient to Cherry Crest Adventure Farm. (The

Strasburg Rail Road

Strasburg Rail Road sells discounted Cherry Crest tickets.) Leaman Place Grove, at the end of the line, appeals to rail fans because it's adjacent to active Amtrak lines. Just don't miss the last train back.

Combo passes good for a train ride and admission to the nearby Railroad Museum of Pennsylvania are available.

Railroad Museum of Pennsylvania

Directly across the street from the Strasburg Rail Road, the **Railroad Museum of Pennsylvania** (300 Gap Rd., Ronks, 717/687-8628, www.rrmuseumpa.org, 9am-5pm Mon.-Sat., noon-5pm Sun., closed Mon. Nov.-Mar., admission $10, seniors $9, children 3-11 $8) boasts a world-class collection of railroad artifacts, including many last-of-their-kind locomotives. Its 100,000-square-foot exhibit hall holds some 50 locomotives and rail cars. Dozens of others reside in the restoration yard, which is open to visitors when weather and staffing permit. The museum offers daily tours of its restoration shop, normally closed to the public for safety reasons. The $10 tour fee directly benefits the museum's efforts to rescue historic railroad equipment from extinction.

Rail fans hoping to find a rare "Big Boy" steam locomotive will be disappointed. The museum, which opened in 1975, is owned and operated by the Pennsylvania Historical and Museum Commission and endeavors to preserve objects relating to the history of railroading in Pennsylvania. The legendary Big Boys didn't ply Pennsylvania's rails. With its 195-ton engine, Pennsylvania Railroad "Mountain" No. 6755 is the largest and heaviest steam locomotive in the museum's collection.

National Toy Train Museum

Real trains are well and good, but there's something enchanting about their much-shrunken kin. Which makes the **National Toy Train Museum** (300 Paradise Ln., Strasburg, 717/687-8976, www.nttmuseum.

org, hours vary by season, admission $7, seniors $6, children 6-12 $4) an exceptionally enchanting place. It houses one of the most extensive collections of toy trains in the world. More than 100 different manufacturers are represented in the museum's collection, which includes some of the earliest and rarest toy trains. It also includes some model trains. The museum, which aspires to look like a Victorian-era station, has five large train layouts.

The museum is operated by the Train Collectors Association, which has its national headquarters there. Those new to "the world's greatest hobby," as the TCA calls it, can learn the ropes via video presentations in the museum. Seasoned collectors can bury their noses in repair guides, trade catalogs, and other materials in the reference library.

Choo Choo Barn

Model train enthusiasts can also find nirvana at the **Choo Choo Barn** (226 Gap Rd., Strasburg, 717/687-7911, www.choochoobarn.com, 10am-5pm daily mid-Mar.-Dec. and select days in Jan., admission $7, children 3-12 $4), which predates the National Toy Train Museum. The family-owned attraction has just one layout: a massive, marvelous display featuring 22 operating trains and more than 150 animated figures and vehicles. Local landmarks including the Strasburg Rail Road and Dutch Wonderland amusement park are represented.

Located next to the Choo Choo Barn, the **Strasburg Train Shop** (717/687-0464, www.etrainshop.com, 10am-5pm daily) caters to the layout builder. It's known as the place to go for uncommon things such as garbage cans.

OTHER SIGHTS
President James Buchanan's Wheatland

The only U.S. president from Pennsylvania lived—and died—on a handsome estate west of downtown Lancaster. James Buchanan, the only bachelor to lead the nation, was secretary of state when he moved to **Wheatland** (230

N. President Ave., Lancaster, 717/392-4633, www.lancasterhistory.org, tours on the hour 10am-3pm Mon.-Sat. Apr.-Oct., hours vary Nov.-Mar., admission $10, seniors $8, children 10 and under free, Yuletide at Wheatland admission $12, children 6-13 $6) in 1848. He announced his 1856 presidential campaign on the front porch of the Federal-style mansion. Reviled for his wishy-washiness on slavery and his handling of the secession crisis, the 15th president penned a defensive memoir after retiring to Wheatland in 1861. His writing desk is among the many artifacts displayed throughout the manse today. The collection includes everything from his White House china to his bathing tub and even a bottle of 1827 Madeira, now half evaporated, from his wine cellar. Buchanan died at his beloved Wheatland in 1868 and is buried at Woodward Hill Cemetery in Lancaster.

Wheatland is part of the campus of LancasterHistory.org, a nonprofit historical organization formed by the 2009 merger of the Lancaster County Historical Society and the James Buchanan Foundation for the Preservation of Wheatland. The campus is also home to an arboretum with more than 100 species of trees. The newly redesigned and expanded **LancasterHistory.org**

headquarters (9:30am-5pm Mon., Wed., and Fri.-Sat., 9:30am-8pm Tues. and Thurs.) has several galleries, which are worth visiting if you're interested in Lancaster County's unique history. Gallery admission is $7 for adults, $5 for seniors and students 11-17. A discount applies when combined with a tour of Wheatland.

Dutch Wonderland

Dutch Wonderland (2249 Lincoln Hwy. E., Lancaster, 717/291-1888, www.dutchwonderland.com) doesn't boast of adrenaline-pumping rides like many amusement parks. Its coaster count has stood at two for more than a decade, and you wouldn't call them hair-raising. The 48-acre park, fronted by a castle facade visible from Route 30, bills itself as "A Kingdom for Kids." In addition to 30-some rides, it offers a variety of live shows daily. They're all quite delightful but none so much as the high-dive shows at Herr's Aqua Stadium. Performers twist, somersault, and splash their way through Disneyesque storylines. Bring swimsuits for Duke's Lagoon, the park's water play area.

Dutch Wonderland is open daily from late May through Labor Day and some weekends before and after that period. Gates open at

President James Buchanan's Wheatland

10am. A variety of admission plans are available. One-day admission is $36.75 for guests ages 3-59, $31.75 for adults 60-69, $23.75 for those 70 and older. Hang on to your ticket stub in case you decide to come back the next day; consecutive-day admission is $28.75. A two-day flex pass, good for visits on any two days during the season, is $52 for anyone 3 or older. If your summer plans also include Hersheypark in nearby Hershey, ask about combo tickets. Hershey Entertainment & Resorts acquired Dutch Wonderland in 2001.

Cherry Crest Adventure Farm

Dutch Wonderland isn't the only must-stop attraction for pint-size visitors to Lancaster County. There's also **Cherry Crest Adventure Farm** (150 Cherry Hill Rd., Ronks, 717/687-6843, www.cherrycrestfarm.com), where every summer a five-acre cornfield is transformed into the Amazing Maize Maze. This maze is no cakewalk. It takes most visitors about an hour to find the exit. But there's no danger of getting hopelessly lost—or bored for that matter. Helpful "Maze Masters" are always on hand, and the paths are peppered with clues and diversions. Open from the week of July 4 though early November, the maze isn't the only attraction on the working farm. Kids can crawl through a hay tunnel, slide down a hay chute on a burlap sack, or hurl pumpkins with giant slingshots. They can ride pedal karts or a tractor-pulled wagon. They can even watch chicks hatch and hold the little fuzzballs. Now that's agritainment.

Cherry Crest is open Saturdays starting Memorial Day weekend; Tuesday-Saturday from the week of July 4 to Labor Day; select days in September; and Thursday-Saturday in October and early November. Admission is $10 before the maze opens and $15-18 afterward, with no charge for children two and under. Cherry Crest, which is not an Amish farm, is just east of Strasburg, less than three miles from the Strasburg Rail Road. In fact, the excursion trains stop at Cherry Crest to pick up and drop off passengers. Cherry Crest sells discounted Strasburg Rail Road tickets.

Kitchen Kettle Village

What started as a home-based jelly-making business has grown into **Kitchen Kettle Village** (3529 Old Philadelphia Pike, Intercourse, 717/768-8261, www.kitchenkettle.com, 9am-6pm Mon.-Sat. May-Oct., 9am-5pm Mon.-Sat. Nov.-Apr.), home to about 40 specialty shops, a pair of restaurants, and a handful of kid-centric attractions. To call it a mall would fail to convey its quaintness. Think of it as a mall in a fairy tale—the sort of place where Snow White would buy ribbons for her hair. The canning kitchen is still the heart of it all. Its repertoire has grown to include not just jellies, jams, and preserves but also relishes, pickles, mustards, salad dressings, grilling sauces, and salsas. All products are made by hand in small batches, and visitors get a front-seat view. (Because the kitchen is staffed by Amish women, photos aren't permitted.) Plenty of visitors have discovered a taste for pickled beets or pepper jam in the **Jam & Relish Kitchen,** which abounds with samples. An attached bakery fills the air with the smells of shoofly pie, whoopie pies, molasses snaps, snickerdoodle cookies, and other local favorites.

Many of the village shops feature locally made foods or goods, including ice cream from a dairy farm just a few miles away, fudge and kettle corn made on-site, fabric bags, quilts, and pottery. The popular **Kling House Restaurant** (8am-3pm Mon.-Thurs., 8am-4pm Fri.-Sat., breakfast $4-9, lunch $8-15) serves the likes of cinnamon-raisin French toast and baked oatmeal for breakfast, a variety of sandwiches, flatbread pizzas, and entrées for lunch, and a killer coconut cream pie. There's also a cafeteria-style restaurant.

The village is home base to **AAA Buggy Rides** (717/989-2829, www.aaabuggyrides.com, 9am-6pm Mon.-Sat. May-Oct., 9am-5pm Mon.-Sat. in Apr. and Nov.), which offers a 35-minute ride ($14, children 3-12 $7) through Amish countryside and a 55-minute ride ($18, children 3-12 $9) that passes over a covered bridge. Other village attractions include pony rides, a petting zoo, and a playground.

Want to stick around after dark? Scattered throughout the village are guest rooms and suites collectively known as **The Inn at Kitchen Kettle Village** ($110-200). Rates include breakfast at the Kling House Restaurant every day except Sunday. Book well in advance if you're coming for the **Rhubarb Festival** (third weekend in May) or another of the village's annual events.

Landis Valley Village & Farm Museum

Born two years apart in the 1860s, brothers Henry and George Landis had a lot in common. Both became engineers. Neither married. They were the kind of people who never threw anything away—the kind who collected things other people regarded as valueless. By 1925 the brothers had amassed so many objects reflective of Pennsylvania German rural life that they opened a small museum on their homestead a few miles north of downtown Lancaster, charging visitors 25 cents apiece. They died a year apart in the 1950s, but the **Landis Valley Village & Farm Museum** (2451 Kissel Hill Rd., Lancaster, 717/569-0401, www.landisvalleymuseum.org, 9am-5pm Mon.-Sat., noon-5pm Sun., admission $12, seniors $10, children 3-11 $8) lives on. Owned by the state since 1953, it has grown into an assemblage of 30-plus historic and re-created buildings housing a collection of more than 100,000 farm, trade, and household artifacts. While some historic buildings are original to the site, including the Landis brothers' 1870s house, many were relocated here over the years. They include a blacksmith shop, a circa 1800 log building that houses exhibits on early printing and leatherworking, and a late 1800s schoolhouse complete with authentic furnishings. Rather than a time capsule of a particular era, Landis Valley is a repository for all things illustrative of Pennsylvania Dutch village and farm life from the mid-1700s to

mid-1900s. Costumed interpreters are often on hand to demonstrate skills such as open-hearth cooking, horse-drawn plowing, tinsmithing, wood carving, and weaving. Heirloom gardens and heritage breed farm animals help bring the past to life. Be sure to stop by the museum store, which features traditional handicrafts.

Landis Valley shares a parking lot with **Hands-on House** (721 Landis Valley Rd., Lancaster, 717/569-5437, www.handson-house.org, 10am-5pm Mon.-Thurs. and Sat., 10am-8pm Fri., noon-5pm Sun. Memorial Day-Labor Day, 11am-4pm Tues.-Thurs., 11am-8pm Fri., 10am-5pm Sat., noon-5pm Sun. Labor Day-Memorial Day, admission $8.50), a museum designed for children 2-10.

Hans Herr House Museum

Built in 1719, the **Hans Herr House** (1849 Hans Herr Dr., Willow Street, 717/464-4438, www.hansherr.org, 9am-4pm Mon.-Sat. Apr.-Nov.) is the oldest structure in Lancaster County and the oldest Mennonite meetinghouse in the Western Hemisphere. Though named for the Mennonite bishop whose flock established the first permanent European settlement in present-day Lancaster County, the stone house was actually built by his son Christian. Today it's the centerpiece of a museum complex that also includes two 19th-century Pennsylvania German farmhouses, several barns and other outbuildings, and a collection of farm equipment spanning three centuries. In 2013 the museum unveiled a replica of a Native American longhouse. The 62-foot-long structure was modeled on remnants of a longhouse excavated locally in 1969. It's one of the country's few replica longhouses—multifamily homes made of logs, saplings, and tree bark.

You can explore the grounds at your own pace—for free—but the Herr House and longhouse can only be seen by guided tour. A 45-minute tour of either structure is $8 for adults, $4 for children 7-12. A combined tour is $15 for adults, $7 for children. Tours begin on the hour. Aficionados of 20th-century

the National Watch & Clock Museum

bowls of water, candles, oil lamps, and incense were used to measure the passage of time.

Perhaps its most impressive holding is a so-called monumental clock made in Hazleton, Pennsylvania, by one Stephen Engle. Designed to awe and amuse audiences, monumental clocks had their heyday in the late 19th century, touring the United States and Europe like so many modern rock stars. Engle spent more than 20 years crafting his 11-foot-tall clock, which has 48 moving figurines and displays such information as month, day of the week, and moon phase along with time. Finishing it around 1878, he entrusted it to promoters who touted it as "The Eighth Wonder of the World" as they hauled it around the eastern United States, charging people to see it. In 1951, after an appearance at the Ohio State Fair, the clock vanished. Members of the National Association of Watch and Clock Collectors spent years hunting for it, finally discovering it in a barn in 1988.

American art may recognize the 1719 house. The great Andrew Wyeth, a descendant of Hans Herr, captured it on canvas before its restoration.

National Watch & Clock Museum

The largest and most comprehensive horological collection in North America can be found in the river town of Columbia, about 10 miles west of Lancaster. Horology is the science of measuring time. Sounds like staid stuff, but a visit to the **National Watch & Clock Museum** (514 Poplar St., Columbia, 717/684-8261, www.nawcc.org, 10am-4pm Tues.-Sat. Dec.-Mar., 10am-5pm Tues.-Sat. and noon-4pm Sun. Apr.-Nov., also open Mon. Memorial Day-Labor Day, admission $8, seniors $7, children 5-16 $4, family $20) will convince you otherwise. Located in the world headquarters of the National Association of Watch and Clock Collectors, the museum traces the history of timekeeping from ancient times to present day. Learn how

Turkey Hill Experience

Like The Hershey Story in Hershey and the Crayola Experience in Easton, the **Turkey Hill Experience** (301 Linden St., Columbia, 888/986-8784, www.turkeyhillexperience. com, admission $9.95, seniors $8.95, children 5-17 $7.95) is a family attraction centered on a consumer brand. Opened in 2011, it tells the story of Turkey Hill Dairy, a Lancaster County-based producer of ice cream and iced tea. It's packed with interactive exhibits. Kids get a huge kick out of milking the mechanical cows and creating their own virtual ice cream flavor. The Taste Lab exhibit, added in 2013, gives visitors the opportunity to turn their virtual ice cream recipe into actual ice cream. The Taste Lab costs an additional $4.55 per person, and reservations are required.

There's no actual production at the Turkey Hill Experience, which occupies a former silk mill in the borough of Columbia, a few blocks from the National Watch & Clock Museum.

Lititz

In a county studded with lovely little towns,

Lititz is generally regarded as the loveliest one of all. Validation came in 2013, when Lititz was named America's Coolest Small Town by *Budget Travel*. The clip-clop of Amish buggies that contributes so much to the appeal of Bird-in-Hand, Intercourse, Strasburg, and other communities west of Lancaster is rarely heard in Lititz. What draws visitors to the borough nine miles north of downtown Lancaster is a combination of historical ambience, boutique shopping, and a busy calendar of events. It doesn't hurt that the smell of chocolate wafts through the streets.

Most of the shops, galleries, eateries, and landmarks lie along East Main Street (Route 772) or Broad Street (Route 501), which meet in the center of town. Be aware that many are closed on Sundays. The second Friday of the month is a great day to visit because merchants pull out all the stops for **Lovin' Lititz Every 2nd** (717/626-6332, www.lititzpa.com, 5pm-9pm), featuring free entertainment and free parking throughout town. Lititz is also a great place to be on Independence Day. First held in 1818, the **4th of July Celebration** (717/626-8981, www.lititzspringspark.org, admission charged) in Lititz Springs Park is the oldest continuous observance of the national holiday. The daylong festivities conclude with

the lighting of thousands of candles and a fireworks show.

Lititz boasts a unique history. It was founded in 1756 by members of the Moravian Church, an evangelical Protestant denomination that originated in the modern-day Czech Republic. For almost 100 years, only Moravians were permitted to live in the village. A group of strict church elders oversaw all aspects of day-to-day life, calling the shots in economic as well as religious matters. After opening its doors to outsiders in the 1850s, Lititz became a stop on the Reading and Columbia Railroad and a summer resort area. Lititz Springs Park and the limestone springs that give it its name were the main attraction. A replica of the passenger depot that stood at the entrance to the park from 1884 to 1957 houses the **Lititz Welcome Center** (18 N. Broad St., 717/626-8981, www.lititzspringspark.org, 10am-4pm Mon.-Sat. and until 8pm on the second Fri. of the month). On the opposite side of the train tracks, which are still used for moving freight, is the **Wilbur Chocolate Company** (48 N. Broad St., 717/626-3249, www.wilburbuds.com, store and museum open 10am-5pm Mon.-Sat., free admission). Founded in 1884 in Philadelphia, based in Lititz since

the Wilbur Chocolate Company

the 1930s, and owned by agribusiness conglomerate Cargill since 1992, Wilbur manufactures chocolate and other ingredients for the baking, candy, and dairy industries. It's best known to consumers for chocolates that resemble a flower bud. (Wilbur Buds also bear a striking resemblance to Hershey's Kisses, which at more than 100 years old aren't quite as old as the squatter Buds.) The factory store offers free samples of the signature confection and a wide selection of other goodies, including fudge, marshmallows, almond bark, and peanut butter meltaways made on the spot. The attached Candy Americana Museum showcases antique candy machinery, cocoa tins, chocolate molds and boxes, marble slabs and rolling pins, and more than 150 porcelain chocolate pots from around the world.

Lititz is also home to a chocolate-centric eatery. **Café Chocolate of Lititz** (40 E. Main St., 717/626-0123, www.chocolatelititz.com, 10:30am-5pm Mon.-Thurs., 9am-9pm Fri.-Sat., 9am-5pm Sun., $6-10) is all about dark chocolate, eschewing varieties with less than 50 percent cocoa solids. The menu draws inspiration from around the globe, which presents a challenge when choosing a bottle to bring to the BYOB. What pairs well with mulligatawny soup, West African peanut chowder, *and* "chili con chocolate" topped with vegan sausage? A chocolate fountain in the front window reminds passersby of the house specialty: dark chocolate fondue.

The food lover's tour of Lititz doesn't end there. Just a couple of blocks from Café Chocolate is the **Julius Sturgis Pretzel Bakery** (219 E. Main St., 717/626-4354, www.juliussturgis.com, 10am-4pm Mon.-Fri. and 9am-5pm Sat. Jan.-mid-Mar., 9am-5pm Mon.-Sat. mid-Mar.-Dec., tour $3.50, children $2.50). Established in 1861, it's regarded as America's first pretzel bakery. Tours include a hands-on lesson in pretzel twisting. The bakery, with its original brick ovens, doesn't do a whole lot of baking these days. Soft pretzels are made in-house, but the many varieties of hard pretzels available in the store come from

Tom Sturgis Pretzels, a Reading-area bakery founded by Julius's grandson.

The sturdy stone house that Julius turned into a pretzel bakery was built in 1784. It's one of more than a dozen 18th-century buildings still in use on East Main Street. Another houses the **Lititz Museum** (145 E. Main St., 717/627-4636, www.lititzhistoricalfoundation. com, 10am-4pm Mon.-Sat. Memorial Day-last Sat. in Oct. and Fri.-Sat. Nov.-Sat. before Christmas, free admission), the place to go for a primer on the town's history. The Lititz Historical Foundation operates the museum and the neighboring **Johannes Mueller House,** which is open for tours ($5, seniors $4, high school students $3) from Memorial Day through the last Saturday in October. Built in 1792, the stone house remains practically unchanged and is furnished with hundreds of artifacts from the late 1700s and early 1800s. The 45-minute tours are led by costumed guides.

Wolf Sanctuary of Pennsylvania

Despite its official-sounding name, the **Wolf Sanctuary** (465 Speedwell Forge Rd., Lititz, 717/626-4617, www.wolfsancpa.com) is not a state facility. It's the pet project of one Lancaster County family, the Darlingtons, with a lot of land and a love for the animal portrayed so harshly in fairy tales. The Darlingtons began taking in wolves and wolf hybrids in the 1980s, after the state forbade keeping them as house pets. Today more than 40 onetime pets—who can't be released into the wild because they rely on humans for food—roam 20-odd acres of the family's property. Walking tours of the fenced refuge are offered Tuesdays, Thursdays, Saturdays, and Sundays. Reservations are required for the weekday tours, which start at 10am and cost $15 for adults, $14 for seniors, and $13 for children 12 and under. You can just show up for weekend tours, offered at 10am June-September and noon October-May. They're $12 for adults, $11 for seniors, and $10 for children. Once a month, on the Saturday closest to the full moon, the sanctuary offers an evening tour (7:30pm, $20, must be 16 or older) complete with campfire and some form of entertainment. Private tours are available by appointment and cost $25 per person. It's best to visit during cold weather, which wolves prefer. On hot days the sanctuary's furry residents are loath to emerge from holes they dig beneath their shelters.

If you're interested in spending hours or even days with the wolves, you're in luck. In 2005 the Darlingtons opened a B&B on their 100-plus acre property, which was the site of an iron forge from the 1760s to 1850s. **Speedwell Forge B&B** (717/626-1760, www. speedwellforge.com, $135-300) offers three guest rooms in what used to be the ironmaster's mansion and three private cottages. The Paymaster's Office cottage, so named because it's where forge employees were paid, is a honeymoon-worthy retreat complete with vaulted ceiling, massive brick fireplace, king-size bed, and in-room whirlpool bath.

Ephrata Cloister

The town of Ephrata, about 15 miles north of downtown Lancaster, is best known as the onetime home of a religious community whose faithful ate meager rations and slept on wooden benches with blocks of wood for pillows. The **Ephrata Cloister** (632 W. Main St., Ephrata, 717/733-6600, www.ephratacloister. org, 9am-5pm Wed.-Sat. and noon-5pm Sun. Jan.-Feb., 9am-5pm Tues.-Sat. and noon-5pm Sun. Mar., 9am-5pm Mon.-Sat. and noon-5pm Sun. Apr.-Oct., 9am-5pm Tues.-Sat. and noon-5pm Sun. Nov.-Dec., admission $10, seniors $9, children 3-11 $6) was the hub of their community and home to members who chose a celibate life. The buildings where white-robed Brothers and Sisters lived, worked, and prayed in the 1700s are now open to the public. At its zenith in the mid-1800s, the community consisted of about 80 celibate members and 200 "householders" who lived on farms around the cloister. The community became known for its Germanic calligraphy, publishing center, and original a cappella music.

Their leader, Conrad Beissel, prescribed a special diet for members of the choir, who sang at an otherworldly high pitch. Today the music composed by Beissel and crew is performed by the Ephrata Cloister Chorus at occasional concerts.

Beissel died in 1768 and was buried in a graveyard on the cloister grounds. His successor wasn't married to the idea of monastic life. After the death of the last celibate member in 1813, householders formed the German Seventh Day Baptist Church. The congregation disbanded in 1934, and several years later the state purchased the cloister property, now a National Historic Landmark. Some of the original buildings, including a worship hall known as the saal, can only be viewed during guided tours, which are offered daily. You can explore other structures on your own.

ENTERTAINMENT AND EVENTS
Performing Arts

Downtown Lancaster is home to one of the oldest theaters in the country. Built in 1852 on the foundation of a pre-Revolutionary prison, the **Fulton Theatre** (12 N. Prince St., Lancaster, 717/397-7425, www.thefulton.org) hosted lectures by Mark Twain and Horace Greeley, performances by Sarah Bernhardt and W. C. Fields, a production of *Ben-Hur* featuring live horses in a spectacular chariot-racing scene (fistfights broke out at the box office when tickets went on sale), and burlesque in its first 100 years. In the 1950s and '60s it served primarily as a movie house. Since then the Fulton has reinvented itself as a producer of professional theater. Productions range from small-cast plays such as *Doubt* to beloved musicals such as *Les Misérables* and *Hello, Dolly!* Each season features a handful of shows designed for pint-size theatergoers. The auditorium, which seats about 700, was restored to its original Victorian splendor in 1995. It's one of a dwindling number still using sandbags and hemp ropes to move scenery. Named for a Lancaster County native credited with developing the first commercially successful steamboat, the Fulton is the primary venue of the **Lancaster Symphony Orchestra** (717/397-7425, www.lancastersymphony.org). Lancaster County has not one but two dinner theaters. In business since 1984, **Rainbow Dinner Theatre** (3065 Lincoln Highway East, Paradise, 717/687-4300, www.rainbowdinnertheatre.com) bills itself as America's only all-comedy dinner theater. It produces several knee-slappers per year, including a Christmas show. The **Dutch Apple Dinner Theatre** (510 Centerville Rd., Lancaster, 717/898-1900, www.dutchapple.com) serves up more shows, and its menu includes dramatic fare such as *Rent*. Both theaters are set back from the road and easily missed. Rainbow is behind the Best Western Plus Revere Inn & Suites on Route 30, about three miles east of the Rockvale Outlets. The Dutch Apple shares a driveway with the Heritage Hotel—Lancaster, just off the Centerville exit of Route 30.

Sight & Sound Theatres

With a theater in Lancaster County and a second in Branson, Missouri, **Sight & Sound Theatres** (800/377-1277, www.sight-sound.com) is the nation's largest Christian theatrical company. Founded in the 1970s by a Lancaster County native, it pulls out all the stops to dramatize biblical stories such as Noah's wet and wild journey, Joseph's journey from slavery to power, and the birth of Jesus. Think elaborate sets and special effects, professional actors and live animals. The Lancaster County **theater** (300 Hartman Bridge Rd., Strasburg) is a vision inside and out. The sprawling, pastel-hued palace features three exterior domes (representing the Trinity), a wraparound stage double the size of Radio City Music Hall's, and one of the largest moving light systems on the East Coast. Four-legged cast members amble to their spots—and "dressing rooms"—via specially designed passageways under the theater floor.

Festivals and Events

What started in 1980 as a jousting demo to draw attention to a new winery has grown into one of Pennsylvania Dutch country's marquee attractions. Jousting is just the tip of the lance at the **Pennsylvania Renaissance Faire** (Mount Hope Estate, 2775 Lebanon Rd., Manheim, 717/665-7021, www.parenfaire.com, admission charged), held weekends August-October. Transported to Elizabethan England, Faire-goers party

the Fulton Theatre

like it's 1589 alongside sword swallowers and fire-breathers, magicians and musicians, jugglers and jesters. The Ren Faire features more than 70 shows per day, including performances of Shakespeare's plays in a three-story replica of London's Globe Theatre. Human pawns, knights, and bishops battle it out on a massive chessboard. Merchants in period costumes demonstrate glassblowing, pottery throwing, leatherworking, bow and arrow making, and more. Even the food vendors wear the clothes and talk the talk of Shakespeare's day as they serve up everything from gelato to giant turkey legs. Though best known for the Ren Faire, Mount Hope Estate hosts a variety of events throughout the year, including murder mystery dinners, a beer festival, and a Celtic festival. Located 15 miles north of Lancaster, the National Register-listed property was home to a prominent iron-making family in the 19th century.

Lancaster's **Long's Park** (1441 Harrisburg Pike, Lancaster, 717/735-8883, www.longspark.org) is another site of much merrymaking. The city park just off Route 30 is a poultry-lover's paradise on the third Saturday of May, when the Sertoma Club of Lancaster holds its annual fundraiser for the park. Members of the civic organization serve more than 25,000 chicken dinners over the course of eight hours. The **Sertoma Chicken BBQ** (717/354-7259, www.lancastersertomabbq.com, admission charged), a tradition since 1953, held the Guinness World Record for most meat consumed at an outdoor event for more than a decade, losing it to a Paraguayan shindig in 2008. June marks the start of the **Long's Park Summer Music Series** (7:30pm Sun. June-Aug.), another decades-old tradition. Bring blankets, lawn chairs, and nibbles for the free concerts. Alcohol isn't permitted in the 80-acre park. The music series is funded in part by proceeds from the **Long's Park Art & Craft Festival** (Labor Day weekend, admission charged), which showcases 200 artists from across the country.

SHOPPING
Outlet Malls

Lancaster County's two outlet malls are just a couple of minutes apart on Route 30. **Rockvale Outlets** (35 S. Willowdale Dr., Lancaster, 717/293-9595, www.rockvaleoutletslancaster.com, 9:30am-9pm Mon.-Sat., 11am-5pm Sun.) features about 100 stores, including Lane Bryant, Jones New York, Pendleton, Casual Male XL, Izod, Gymboree, and Disney Store. It's a great place to shop for the home, counting Pottery Barn, Lenox, and Corningware Corelle Revere among its tenants.

Tanger Outlets (311 Stanley K. Tanger Blvd., Lancaster, 717/392-7260, www.tangeroutlet.com, 9am-9pm Mon.-Sat., 10am-6pm Sun.), located across Route 30 from Dutch Wonderland amusement park, is smaller but chicer, offering designer brands such as Polo Ralph Lauren, Kenneth Cole, Calvin Klein, Brooks Brothers, Coach, and Movado.

"Antiques Capital USA"

Located just off exit 286 of the Pennsylvania Turnpike, the little burg of Adamstown has made a big name for itself in antiquing circles. It's crowded with antiques shops, malls, and markets, most of which can be found along North Reading Road (Route 272). Sundays are a big day in "Antiques Capital USA." That's when **Renninger's Antiques Market** and the **Black Angus Antiques Mall** are open. The former (2500 N. Reading Rd., Denver, 717/336-2177, www.renningers.com, indoor market 7:30am-4pm Sun., outdoor market opens at 5am) features 375 dealers indoors and, weather permitting, hundreds more outdoors. Bring a flashlight to get in on the early morning action.

The 70,000-square-foot **Black Angus Antiques Mall** (2800 N. Reading Rd., Adamstown, 717/484-4386, www.stoudts.com, mall 7:30am-4pm Sun., outdoor pavilions 5:30am-noon) is part of a sprawling complex of attractions operated by husband and wife Ed and Carol Stoudt. More than 300 dealers set up shop inside the mall, selling everything from fine art and early American furniture to tools and small collectibles. About 100 more can be found outside. At 1pm, take a break from shopping for a free tour of **Stoudt's Brewing Company.** Frequent visitors to Europe, the Stoudts established the microbrewery in 1987 with the goal of making an authentic German-style beer. And they succeeded: Gold Lager and Pils, the brewery's German-style flagship beers, have racked up awards and accolades. Brewery tours, also offered at 3pm Saturdays, meet in the lobby of the adjacent **Black Angus Restaurant & Pub,** which specializes in steaks. Its breads are made in the **Wonderful Good Market** (9am-4pm Fri.-Sun.), the Stoudts' bakery, creamery, and specialty foods store.

Adamstown offers plenty of antiquing on days other than Sunday. **Heritage Antique Center** (2750 N. Reading Rd., Adamstown, 717/484-4646, www.heritageantiquecenter. com), one of the area's oldest antiques stores, and the **Antiques Showcase & German Trading Post** (2152 N. Reading Rd., Denver, 717/336-8847, www.blackhorselodge.com), with nearly 300 showcases full of fine antiques and collectibles, are open seven days a week. Not to be missed: **The Country French Collection** (2887 N. Reading Rd.,

Adamstown, 717/484-0200, www.country-frenchantiques.com, noon-5pm Sat.-Sun. and by appointment), which imports 18th- and 19th-century antiques from France and England and restores them to pristine condition.

Adamstown's antiquing scene goes into overdrive during **Antique Extravaganza** (www.antiquescapital.com), held each April, June, and September. Outside markets mushroom and inside markets keep longer hours during the four-day event, which attracts dealers from across the country.

Mud Sales

Held at fire companies throughout Lancaster County, "mud sales" are a chance to get dirt-cheap prices on everything from antiques to aluminum siding, lawn equipment to livestock, homemade food to horse carriages. Teeming as they are with Amish and Mennonite buyers and sellers, these fundraising sales/auctions are also a cultural immersion experience. Why are they called mud sales? Because many take place in the spring, when the ground is thawing—though it's not unusual for fire companies to hold mud sales in summer or fall. Visit www.padutchcountry.com or call 717/299-8901 for a schedule of mud sales.

Black Angus Antiques Mall

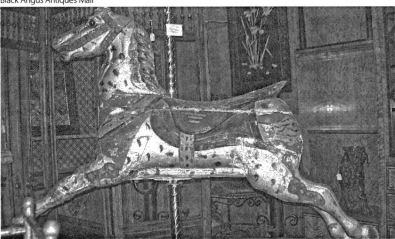

Quilts and Fabrics

Mud sales are great places to buy locally crafted quilts, but if your visit to Lancaster County doesn't coincide with one, you're not out of luck. Quilt shops are more common than stoplights in the Amish countryside. Most sell a variety of handicrafts. (This author's fave: the ingenious pillow-blanket hybrid known as the "quillow.") Many are home-based businesses, allowing shoppers a glimpse into the everyday lives of locals. Just about all quilt shops are closed on Sundays. The **Quilt Shop at Miller's** (2811 Lincoln Highway East, Ronks, 717/687-8439, www.quiltshopatmillers.com, open Wed.-Sun. Jan.-Feb., daily Mar.-Dec.) is an exception. It's right next to the popular Miller's Smorgasbord on Route 30, about a mile and a half east of Route 896.

Intercourse is a good place to start a quilt shopping spree. The village along Route 340 (Old Philadelphia Pike) is home to **The Old Country Store** (800/828-8218, www.theoldcountrystore.com, open Mon.-Sat.), stocked with thousands of items made by local craftspeople, most of them Amish or Mennonite. In addition to hundreds of quilts, it carries potholders and pottery, Christmas ornaments and cornhusk bunnies, faceless Amish dolls and darling stuffed bears, pillows of various sizes and paper cuttings known as *scherenschnitte*. With its selection of more than 6,000 bolts of fabric, the store is as much a starting point for needlecraft projects as a showplace for finished products. Quilt books, color-coordinated fabric packs, and pattern kits are also on offer. There's a quilt museum on the second floor of the store. It's best known for showcasing antique Amish and Mennonite quilts but has also mounted exhibitions of contemporary quilts, African American quilts, and antebellum album quilts.

In the complex of shops known as Kitchen Kettle Village is the airy **Village Quilts** (3529 Old Philadelphia Pike, Intercourse, 717/768-2787, www.kitchenkettle.com/quilts, open Mon.-Sat.), which commissions works from a select group of home quilters. Each masterpiece is signed and dated and comes with a certificate for insurance purposes. The shop offers one-on-one quilting instruction ($80 for 90 minutes) by appointment.

A few minutes east of Intercourse along Route 340 is **Esh's Handmade Quilts** (3829 Old Philadelphia Pike, Gordonville, 717/768-8435, open Mon.-Sat.), an Amish-owned shop on an operating dairy farm. And a few minutes west of Intercourse is **The Quilt & Fabric Shack** (3137 Old Philadelphia Pike, Bird-In-Hand, 717/768-0338, www.thequiltandfabricshack.com, open Mon.-Sat.), boasting four rooms of fabrics. Its "bargain room" has hundreds of bolts priced at $4-5 per yard. Just northwest of Intercourse along Route 772, **Family Farm Quilts** (3511 W. Newport Rd., 717/768-8375, www.familyfarmquilts.com, open Mon.-Sat.) counts more than 200 local women among its quilt suppliers. Its selection of handicrafts includes purses made of antique quilts, place mats, chair pads, children's toys, and baskets.

Witmer Quilt Shop (1076 W. Main St., New Holland, 717/656-9526, open Mon.-Tues. and Thurs.-Sat.), located five miles north of Intercourse along Route 23, is remarkable for its selection of lovingly restored antique quilts. Emma Witmer's shop/home is also stocked with more than 100 new quilts, many in patterns she herself designed. Give her a few months and she'll give you a custom quilt.

As you make your way between quilt shops, keep your eyes peeled for handmade "quilts sold here" signs inviting you to pull into a drive and knock on the door.

Susquehanna Glass Factory Outlet and Tour

Founded in 1910, **Susquehanna Glass** (731 Ave. H, Columbia, 717/684-2155, www.susquehannaglass.com, store open 9am-5pm Tues.-Sat., tours 10:30am and 1pm Tues. and Thurs., reservations required) counts retailers Williams-Sonoma, Restoration Hardware, and David's Bridal among its customers. The glass decorator best known for personalized products offers everything from storage jars to lead crystal bowls at its factory store, located half a mile from the National Watch & Clock Museum in the Susquehanna River town of Columbia. Tours of the factory, where glass is still cut by hand, are offered year-round except when temps creep into the 90s. The tours are free and last 30-45 minutes.

ACCOMMODATIONS

Lancaster County has lodging options aplenty. Its hotels and motels run the gamut from major brands such as Holiday Inn, Comfort Inn, and Travelodge to unique independents such as the **Red Caboose** (312 Paradise Ln., Ronks, 717/687-5000, www.redcaboosemotel.com, $70-160), a motel made of historic train cars and cabooses, and the 97-room **Fulton Steamboat Inn** (Routes 30 and 896, Lancaster, 717/299-9999, www.fultonsteamboatinn.com, $80-180), built to resemble a steamboat and named for a Lancaster County native who pioneered steam-powered shipping. Travelers who prefer bed-and-breakfasts can take their pick of more than 150. Indeed, Lancaster County has more B&Bs than any place on the East Coast except Cape Cod. They're a diverse bunch: Bed down in an 18th-century stone house, an elegant Victorian manse, or on a working farm. If you travel with young children, you probably eschew B&Bs, but a farm stay is a different animal (hardy har har). It's lodging, education, and entertainment rolled into one—assuming you find gathering eggs and bottle-feeding calves entertaining. A list of Lancaster County farms that offer overnight accommodations is available at www.afarmstay.com.

The **Pennsylvania Dutch Convention & Visitors Bureau** (717/299-8901, www.padutchcountry.com) is a good source of information about lodging options. Its website allows for searches by lodging type and price range. The **Mennonite Information Center** (2209 Millstream Rd., Lancaster, 717/299-0954, www.mennoniteinfoctr.com) maintains a list of Mennonite-owned guesthouses, available at the center and on its website.

Under $100

Located next to Dutch Wonderland amusement park, **Old Mill Stream Campground** (2249 Lincoln Hwy. E., Lancaster, 717/299-2314, www.oldmillstreamcampground.com, campsite $37-49, mobile home rental $100-180, open Apr.-Dec.) makes a great home base for families with young children. The 15-acre campground has more than 160 tent and RV sites, a game room, a country store, laundry rooms, and free wireless Internet access.

The **Carriage House Motor Inn** (144 E. Main St., Strasburg, 717/687-7651, www.carriagehousemotorinn.net, $60-110) is a good noncamping option in this price range. It's walking distance from the Railroad Museum of Pennsylvania and the Strasburg Rail Road, which makes it appealing to rail fans. Families will appreciate its three-room suite. Rates include a continental breakfast. For about the same price, you can spend the night at nearby **Rayba Acres Farm** (183 Black Horse Rd., Paradise, 717/687-6729, www.raybaacres.com, $85-90) or **Neffdale Farm** (604 Strasburg Rd., Paradise, 717/687-7837, www.neffdale-farm.com, $80), both Mennonite-owned.

$100-150

Located just off Route 30 west of Lancaster city, the **Heritage Hotel—Lancaster** (500 Centerville Rd., Lancaster, 800/223-8963, www.heritagelancaster.com, $90-180) is a great choice for nightlife-loving travelers. **Loxley's** (717/898-2431), its restaurant and bar, attracts locals and hotel guests alike. Named for Robin of Loxley, the archer and outlaw better known as Robin Hood, it boasts a two-level deck that looks like a giant tree house. The hotel has 166 standard-looking guest rooms, a business center, a fitness room, and an outdoor pool. The Dutch Apple Dinner Theatre is right next door.

Sleep under handmade quilts and awake to the clip-clop of Amish buggies at **The Inn at Kitchen Kettle Village** (3529 Old Philadelphia Pike, Intercourse, 717/768-8261, www.kitchenkettle.com, $110-200). Scattered throughout the uber-quaint village, accommodations range from standard rooms to two-bedroom suites that sleep up to six. Guests enjoy a free breakfast at the on-site Kling House Restaurant Monday-Saturday.

Breakfast at ★ **Verdant View Farm B&B** (429 Strasburg Rd., Paradise, 717/687-7353, www.verdantview.com, $70-120), one mile east of Strasburg on Route 741, begins with a joining of hands and a rendition of the Johnny Appleseed song (*Oh, the Lord's been good to me . . .*). It's not unusual for two, three, or even four generations of the Ranck family, which has operated the 118-acre dairy and crop farm for almost a century, to join guests around the table, set with pitchers of raw milk, platters of farm-fresh meat and eggs, and homemade pies. Breakfast isn't the first thing on the menu at Verdant View. Guests can begin the day with a farm tour, complete with opportunities to milk a cow, frolic with kittens, and feed calves, goats, bunnies, and other animals. Verdant View also offers tractor-pulled wagon rides and "farmer's apprentice" programs in topics as diverse as making cheese and artificially inseminating cows. (Breakfast and some farm experiences aren't offered on Sundays, when the Rancks attend their Mennonite church.) The nine guest rooms, spread between an 1896 farmhouse and the "little white house" down the lane, are nothing fancy. But what it lacks in frills the B&B more than makes up for in hospitality.

The charming town of Lititz has several recommendable accommodations in this price range. Chief among them is the **General Sutter Inn** (14 E. Main St., Lititz, 717/626-2115, www.generalsutterinn.com, $70-225), which offers 16 rooms and suites in two radically different styles. Ten are decorated in a Victorian style. The third floor, known as the Rock Lititz Penthouse, features edgy, rock-inspired décor, including curtain rods fashioned from microphone stands and a signed poster from singer Roger Daltrey of The Who. More than 200 years old, the inn took its present name in the 1930s to honor John Augustus Sutter, who established a settlement in California in the 1840s, saw it overrun by gold-seekers, and lived his final years in Lititz. Guests enjoy a complimentary continental breakfast. The **Alden House Bed & Breakfast** (62 E. Main St., Lititz, 717/627-3363, www.aldenhouse.com, $110-160), with seven guest rooms and suites, is another fine choice in the center of town. Its breakfast is a multicourse affair.

Over $150

Visitors to downtown Lancaster may find it hard to believe that the **Lancaster Marriott at Penn Square** (25 S. Queen St., Lancaster, 717/239-1600, www.lancastermarriott.com, $150-300) and adjoining Lancaster County Convention Center opened in 2009. The 19-floor hotel smack-dab in the center of town looks mighty historical. That's because developers incorporated the Beaux Arts facade of a shuttered century-old department store into its design. A contemporary aesthetic takes over in the soaring lobby and spacious rooms. The hotel boasts an indoor pool and a spa (717/207-4076, www.mandarinrosespa.com). The on-site **Penn Square Grille and Rendezvous Lounge** (717/207-4033, www.pennsquaregrille.com) offer contemporary American cuisine and 30 wines by the glass. Central Market, the Fulton Theatre, the Demuth Museum, and other downtown attractions are just a skip and a jump away. On the downside: On-site parking is $18 per day ($30 if you go the valet route), and in-room Internet access will set you back $12.95 per day.

With its brick walls and wood beams, locally crafted furnishings and flat-screen TVs, art gallery and all-natural restaurant, the ★ **Lancaster Arts Hotel** (300 Harrisburg Ave., 717/299-3000, www.lancasterartshotel.com, $180-360) is the city's hippest lodging property by a mile. "Hip" implies new, but the building itself dates to the late 1800s. Built as a tobacco warehouse, it found a new life as a boutique hotel in 2006. Original works by area artists adorn each of 63 guest rooms and suites, some of which boast in-room whirlpools. Amenities include 24-hour business and fitness centers, bicycle rentals, and free parking. Internet access and a continental breakfast are also on the house. **John J. Jeffries** (717/431-3307, www.johnjjeffries.com), the on-site restaurant and lounge, bills itself as the leading consumer of local organic meats and vegetables in central Pennsylvania. Happy hour is 4pm-6pm daily.

Located midway between the villages of Intercourse and Bird-in-Hand on Route 340, ★ **AmishView Inn & Suites** (3125 Old Philadelphia Pike, Bird-in-Hand, 866/735-1600, www.amishviewinn.com, $125-350) is right in the heart of Amish country. Rooms on the backside of the hotel boast farmland views, and it's not unusual to spot a farmer working his fields with horse-drawn equipment or Amish children heading to school. That's not the only thing it has going for it. AmishView has an indoor pool and whirlpool, a fitness center, an arcade room, and a guest laundry. Its 50 guest rooms and suites feature mahogany furniture, kitchenettes, DVD players, and free high-speed Internet access. Suites have fireplaces and/or whirlpools. A complimentary country breakfast complete with made-to-order omelets and waffles is served every morning. Plain & Fancy Farm Restaurant, one of the region's most popular Pennsylvania Dutch eateries, is just outside the doors.

FOOD

Leave your diet at the Lancaster County line. Visiting this corner of the globe without indulging in a Pennsylvania Dutch-style meal is like visiting Disney World and not riding the rides. The cuisine is anything but light, and unless you seek out a restaurant with an à la carte menu (wussy), you're looking at an all-you-can-eat experience. Approach it with the abandon you bring to Thanksgiving dinner. If you don't stuff yourself silly, you're sort of missing the point. This is the food of hardworking farm families. This is no time to turn down seconds.

It would be unwise to fill up on Pennsylvania Dutch foods meal after meal, not only because of the effect on your waistline but because Lancaster County has some excellent non-Deutsch eateries. You can find everything from crepes to authentic Cajun cuisine within its borders. The city of Lancaster, in particular, is undergoing a restaurant boom.

Pennsylvania Dutch Fare

If you're new to Pennsylvania Dutch cuisine, you should know a few things. Around here, **chicken pot pie** isn't a pie at all. It's a stew with square-cut egg noodles. A **whoopie pie** isn't a pie either. Think of it as a dessert burger: creamy icing pressed between two bun-shaped cakes. Chocolate cake with white icing is most common, but you'll also encounter variations such as pumpkin cake with cream cheese icing. The annual **Whoopie Pie Festival** (Hershey Farm Restaurant & Inn, Rte. 896, Strasburg, 717/687-8635, www.whoopiepiefestival.com, early Sept., free) features more than 100 varieties. Pennsylvania Dutch country's most iconic dessert, the **shoofly pie,** is, in fact, a pie with a crumb crust. But it's nothing like the fruit or cream pies served at diners throughout the country. Packed with molasses and brown sugar, the joltingly sweet treat comes in "wet bottom" and "dry bottom" varieties. A wet-bottomed shoofly pie is more gooey and molasses-y than its dry-bottomed cousin. Other regional specialties include egg noodles with browned butter, **chow-chow** (a pickled vegetable relish), **scrapple** (a breakfast food made with pork scraps), and **schnitz un knepp** (a dish consisting of dried apples, dumplings, and ham).

Lancaster County's most popular Pennsylvania Dutch restaurants generally fall into one of two categories: smorgasbord and family-style. With seating for 1,200 and a seemingly endless array of dishes, ★ **Shady Maple Smorgasbord** (129 Toddy Dr., East Earl, 717/354-8222, www.shady-maple.com/smorgasbord, 5am-8pm Mon.-Sat.) is the behemoth of the bunch. Don't be surprised to find a waiting line. On Saturday evenings it can take upwards of an hour to get seated. You really need to see this place to appreciate its enormity. Lunch and dinner buffets feature everything from Pennsylvania Dutch dishes to pizza to fajitas. Save room for dozens of dessert options. Lunch is $13 on weekdays, $19 on Saturday. Dinner is $18-24, depending on the day's specials. Seniors enjoy a 10 percent discount, and children 4-10 eat for half price. (Anyone who has recently undergone a gastric bypass operation also gets a discount.) Shady Maple's breakfast buffet ($10 weekdays, $12 Saturday) gets high marks from scrapple fans. A breakfast menu (under $10) is available on weekdays.

Bird-in-Hand Family Restaurant & Smorgasbord (2760 Old Philadelphia Pike, Bird-in-Hand, 717/768-1500, www.bird-in-hand.com, 6am-8pm Mon.-Sat., breakfast buffet $9, lunch buffet $12-14, dinner buffet $16-19, age-based pricing for children 4-12) offers both menu and smorgasbord dining for breakfast, lunch, and dinner. Its kids buffet is designed to look like Noah's Ark, complete with stuffed animals peering through the portholes. If you enjoy the baked goods, stop by the **Bird-in-Hand Bakery** (2715 Old Philadelphia Pike, Bird-in-Hand, 800/524-3429, www.bird-in-hand.com, 6am-6pm Mon.-Fri., 6am-5pm Sat.) and take some home. It's just down the road. Specialties include soft potato rolls, red velvet cake, and apple dumplings.

Hershey Farm Restaurant (240 Hartman Bridge Rd., Ronks, 717/687-8635, www.hersheyfarm.com, 8am-8pm Mon.-Fri. and 7am-8pm Sat.-Sun., closed Sun. evenings and Mon. Nov.-Apr., breakfast buffet $11, lunch/dinner buffet $17-26, age-based pricing for children 4-12) also offers a choice of menu or smorgasbord dining. The on-site bakery is known for its whoopie pies (Hershey Farm hosts the Whoopie Pie Festival) and triple-layer chocolate cake. A chocolate fountain graces the dessert bar on evenings and weekends. **Miller's Smorgasbord** (2811 Lincoln Hwy. East, Ronks, 717/687-6621, www.millerssmorgasbord.com, breakfast 7:30am-10:30am Sat.-Sun. year-round, lunch/dinner

from 11:30am daily early Mar.-Dec., dinner from 4pm Mon.-Thurs. and lunch/dinner from 11:30am Fri.-Sun. Jan.-early Mar., breakfast buffet $11, lunch/dinner buffet $24, age-based pricing for children 4-12) is unusual in that it serves alcohol, including cocktails made with its own shoofly liqueur. Menu dining is available during lunch and dinner.

★ **Plain & Fancy Farm Restaurant** (3121 Old Philadelphia Pike, Bird-in-Hand, 717/768-4400, www.plainandfancyfarm.com, lunch/dinner from 11:30am daily Mar.-Dec., closed Jan.-Feb.) is Lancaster County's oldest and arguably best destination for family-style dining. Most family-style restaurants in Pennsylvania Dutch country follow a similar recipe: guests are seated—often at tables with other parties—and brought platters of food, which are replenished until everyone is sated. Plain & Fancy's "Amish farm feast" ($20 per person, children 4-12 $10) features made-from-scratch fried chicken, baked sausage, chicken pot pie with homemade noodles, real mashed potatoes, and more. The restaurant, which opened in 1959, also offers an à la carte menu. Its signature dessert, sour cream apple crumb pie, is out of this world. Though it seats 700, you'd be wise to make a reservation. It's more popular than ever after being featured in an episode of the Travel Channel's *Man v. Food Nation*.

Lancaster

With a wide variety of cuisines represented under one roof, **Central Market** (23 N. Market St., 717/735-6890, www.centralmarketlancaster.com, 6am-4pm Tues. and Fri., 6am-2pm Sat.) is one of downtown Lancaster's most popular lunch spots. You'll find vendors selling everything from made-to-order salads to homemade rice pudding. Ethnic options include Narai Exotic Thai Cuisine (get there early for the hot-selling fresh spring rolls) and Saife's Middle Eastern Food. The downsides: Central Market is open just three days a week, and seating is limited.

More upscale dining options abound. Lancaster County native Tim Carr lent his culinary talents to area country clubs before putting his name to a restaurant. Spitting distance from Central Market, **Carr's Restaurant** (50 W. Grant St., 717/299-7090, www.carrsrestaurant.com, lunch 11:30am-2:30pm Tues.-Sat., brunch 11:30am-2:30pm Sun., dinner 5:30pm-9:30pm Tues.-Thurs. and 5:30pm-10pm Fri.-Sat., lunch/brunch $9-20, dinner $14-32) puts a sophisticated spin on comfort foods, e.g., mac and cheese loaded with Maine lobster chunks. Request a table near the back of the basement-level restaurant, where a glass wall affords a view of the wine cellar. You're welcome to bring your own bottle (a $15 corkage fee applies), but the selection here is one of the best in town. In 2009 Carr opened **Crush Wine Bar** (4:30pm-9:30pm Tues.-Thurs., 4:30pm-10pm Fri.-Sat.) above his restaurant. On offer: 20-odd wines by the glass and half glass, a carefully curated assortment of beers, several kinds of absinthe, and creative tapas.

A short stroll away, German-born chef Gunter Backhaus presides over **The Loft** (201 W. Orange St., 717/299-0661, www.theloftlancaster.com, lunch 11:30am-2pm Mon.-Fri., dinner 5:30pm-9pm Mon.-Sat., lunch $9-14, dinner $16-34), locally famous for its jumbo shrimp cocktail. Backhaus doesn't shy away from the likes of frog legs, snails, and alligator tails, but timid palates needn't fear. The menu also features rosemary roasted free-range chicken, filet mignon, and lobster. Cozy and unpretentious, the restaurant gets its name from the open-beam ceiling in one of two dining rooms.

It's not just dieters who sup on salad at the **Belvedere Inn** (402 N. Queen St., 717/394-2422, www.belvederelancaster.com, lunch 11am-2pm Mon.-Fri., dinner 5pm-11pm Sun.-Thurs. and 5pm-midnight Fri.-Sat., bar open until 2am daily, lunch $7-14, dinner $12-32). The grilled Caesar salad at this elegant restaurant is a thing of legend. Have it plain or choose from toppings including tenderloin tips, sautéed scallops, and grilled salmon. A petite version is available at dinnertime, when entrées such as wild boar Bolognese

and gnocchi with Maine lobster vie for attention. **Crazy Shirley's** (7pm-2am Wed.-Thurs., 5pm-2am Fri.-Sat.), a piano bar and lounge on the second floor of the Belvedere, hosts karaoke every Wednesday and DJs Thursday-Saturday.

The classic and seasonal cocktails at **Checkers Bistro** (300 W. James St., 717/509-1069, www.checkersbistro.com, 11:30am-2:30pm and 4:30pm-10pm Tues.-Fri., 11:30am-10pm Sat., 4pm-9pm Sun., lunch $9-17, dinner $20-34) bode well for the meal ahead. "Classic and seasonal" also describe the food menu, which includes fish-and-chips, steak frites, and grilled pizzas with toppings such as lobster, pine nuts, prosciutto, and fig. The small plates menu is particularly appealing, with options both common (chicken wings) and singular (Peking duck tacos).

Like Checkers, ★ **FENZ Restaurant & Latenight** (398 Harrisburg Ave., Ste. 100, 717/735-6999, www.fenzrestaurant.com, dinner from 5pm Mon.-Sat., lounge opens at 4pm, $14-28) excels in cocktails and small plates. Give the pickle fries a chance: the tempura-battered kosher dill spears are positively addictive. Stylishly appointed with a clientele to match, FENZ has two levels with a bar on each. The upstairs has a livelier, more youthful vibe. Take a seat at the downstairs bar to watch the chef at work. The menu is mindful of vegetarians and vegans. FENZ is housed in a 19th-century foundry. Don't waste time searching for street parking. There's a lot behind the building, accessible from Charlotte Street.

A discussion of Lancaster's fine dining scene wouldn't be complete without words of praise for **Gibraltar** (931 Harrisburg Ave., 717/397-2790, www.kearesrestaurants.com/gibraltar, lunch 11:30am-2:30pm Mon.-Fri., dinner 5pm-10pm Mon.-Thurs., 5pm-10:30pm Fri.-Sat., 5pm-9:30pm Sun., bar open as late as 2am, lunch $8-19, dinner $19-34), with its Mediterranean-influenced cuisine, *Wine Spectator*-lauded wine list, and gracious service. The seafood is simply phenomenal.

Start off with selections from the raw bar or an order of steamed mussels and proceed to entrées like whole Adriatic Sea branzino (European sea bass), rainbow trout stuffed with crab, and Moroccan spiced colossal shrimp. A tapas menu is available for those in the sharing spirit. Save room for a house-made pastry.

Strasburg

Strasburg, with its train-related attractions and proximity to the Sight & Sound theater, sees large numbers of tourists. But its restaurants feel refreshingly untouristy. Smack-dab in the center of town, the **Strasburg Country Store & Creamery** (1 W. Main St., 717/687-0766, www.strasburg.com, open daily, hours vary) is best known as a destination for dessert and a dose of nostalgia. But it also offers deli fare, including Reuben sandwiches, cheeseburgers, and hot dogs—all served with locally made potato chips. Cross your fingers that the day's specials include a bread bowl filled with Pennsylvania Dutch-style chicken corn soup. As for dessert, choose from 20-plus flavors of ice cream and mix-ins such as M&M's and granola. A wide variety of chocolate-covered goodies vie for attention with fudge, peanut brittle, and

caramel corn. Have a seat inside to soak in the old-timey touches, from vintage Cream of Wheat posters to a 19th-century marble soda fountain. Have a seat outside to watch horse-drawn buggies negotiating the intersection of Routes 741 and 896.

Purchased in 2003 by a couple with no experience in food service, ★ **The Iron Horse Inn** (135 E. Main St., 717/687-6362, www.ironhorsepa.com, noon-9pm Mon. and Wed., noon-10pm Thurs.-Sat., noon-7pm Sun., lunch $7-10, dinner $9-42) has emerged as one of those rare restaurants that pair fine food with a casual ambience. Denise Waller, one-half of the ownership team and a nurse by training, buys broccoli, squash, potatoes, and other produce directly from local Amish farmers, shrinking the field-to-table timeline to a few hours in some cases. Lunch at the Iron Horse (a Native American term for trains) can be as simple as a grilled ham and cheddar sandwich or as sophisticated as crepes stuffed with lump crabmeat. The asparagus fries—that's right: deep-fried spears of asparagus—go well with any dish. Dinner options range from the "Strasburger" to German/Austrian specialties to vegetable stir-fry. The lineup of draft beers features local brews along with German imports, and the wine list includes

the Strasburg Country Store & Creamery

selections from Twin Brook Winery, about 10 miles east of Strasburg.

Just east of town on Route 741 is an outpost of regional chain **Isaac's Restaurant & Deli** (226 Gap Rd., 717/687-7699, www.isaacsdeli.com, 10am-9pm Mon.-Thurs., 10am-10pm Fri.-Sat., 11am-9pm Sun., call for winter hours, $6-12). The Strasburg location, which shares an address with the Choo Choo Barn, a model railroader's mecca, boasts a dining area decked out like a train car. Its repertoire of made-from-scratch soups is 200 strong, but only the delicious creamy pepperjack tomato is available every day. The long list of sandwiches includes half a dozen veggie options. Pretzel sandwiches like the Salty Eagle (grilled ham, Swiss cheese, mustard) and Mallard (roast beef, bacon, mushrooms, melted cheddar, mild horseradish sauce) are particularly popular. You'll also find Isaac's in downtown Lancaster (25 N. Queen St., 717/394-5544), Lititz (4 Crosswinds Rd., 717/625-1181), and Ephrata (120 N. Reading Rd., 717/733-7777), among other places.

Lititz

The historic **General Sutter Inn** (14 E. Main St., 717/626-2115, www.generalsutterinn.com), located at the junction of Route 501 and East Main Street in the heart of Lititz, offers dining as well as accommodations. The elegant restaurant (11am-3pm Mon., 11am-3pm and 5pm-9pm Tues.-Thurs., 11am-3pm and 5pm-9:30pm Fri., 8am-9:30pm Sat., 11am-9pm Sun., $10-33) isn't as pricey as its white tablecloths suggest. Its menu includes burgers and sandwiches as well as loftier fare such as filet mignon and roasted half duck. The crab cakes sell like hotcakes. Alfresco dining is available during the warmer months. In 2010 the inn unveiled a British-style pub, **Bulls Head Public House** (11:30am-11pm Sun.-Thurs., 11:30am-midnight Fri.-Sat., kitchen closes at 9:30pm Sun.-Thurs. and 10pm Fri.-Sat.), which offers the same menu. Beer lovers are bonkers for the place, which boasts more than a dozen rotating drafts and 80-plus bottles.

Columbia

Order the whoopie pie at ★ **Prudhomme's Lost Cajun Kitchen** (50 Lancaster Ave., 717/684-1706, www.lostcajunkitchen.com, 4:30pm-11pm Mon., 11am-11pm Tues.-Thurs., 11am-midnight Fri.-Sat., 11am-9pm Sun., $4-22) and what you'll get is a far cry from the classic Pennsylvania Dutch dessert. In place of the mound-shaped cakes: homemade cornbread. In place of the icing center: tender crabmeat. Served with a side of creamy mushroom sauce, the appetizer is a Lost Cajun original. Owners David and Sharon Prudhomme—he of Louisiana, she of New Jersey—brought their brand of Cajun cooking to Pennsylvania Dutch country in 1992. The name Prudhomme should not be unfamiliar to foodies. David's uncle, Paul Prudhomme, owner of K-Paul's Louisiana Kitchen in New Orleans, is widely credited with popularizing Cajun cuisine. David learned the ropes in the restaurant his uncle opened in 1979. He makes just about everything from scratch—from salad dressings to the turkey andouille sausage that flavors his jambalaya—and still finds time to work the front of the house, where Sharon presides. Adventurous eaters delight in the menu, which includes turtle soup, alligator tail, and deep-fried bison testicles. But what Lost Cajun does best is blackened catfish. Try the melt-in-your-mouth catfish nuggets or the Cajun-meets-Mexican catfish fajita. The casual, playfully decorated restaurant and bar is also famous for its oversized onion rings. You'll need a knife and fork to attack these bad boys.

Mount Joy

Bube's Brewery (102 N. Market St., 717/653-2056, www.bubesbrewery.com) is reason enough to visit the town of Mount Joy, which at 14 miles northwest of Lancaster isn't particularly close to major tourist attractions. The one-of-a-kind Bube's is many things. For starters, it's a trip back in time. Listed in the National Register of Historic Places, the large brewery/restaurant complex looks much as it did in the late 1800s, when German immigrant Alois Bube produced lager beers there. Bube died in 1908, and the buildings were largely untouched until 1968, when restoration work began. Today they house a microbrewery, several restaurants, a gift shop, and an art gallery. Occupying the original bottling plant is the **Bottling Works** (lunch from 11am Mon.-Sat. and noon Sun., dinner from 5pm daily, $6-29), most casual of the restaurants. Its menu is typical of brewpubs: plenty of deep-fried munchies, soups and salads, burgers and sandwiches, and a selection of hearty entrées. Open-air dining is available in the adjacent **Biergarten,** where you'll find the huge boiler that created steam to power Mr. Bube's brewery.

It's best to make a reservation if you're keen on dining more than 40 feet below ground in the **Catacombs** (dinner from 5:30pm weekdays and 5pm weekends, $22-45). The fine dining restaurant in the original brewery's stone-walled cellars offers the likes of roast duckling, crabmeat-stuffed lobster tail, and filet mignon amid candlelight. On most Sundays it serves a themed feast with a heaping side of theatrics. Bawdy medieval-themed feasts are most common, but its repertoire also includes Roman-, pirate-, and fairy-themed feasts, Halloween-themed feasts in October, and Christmas-themed feasts in December. Feast tickets must be purchased in advance.

Bube's also offers murder mystery dinners ($45) and ghost tours ($10, restaurant guests $5).

INFORMATION

The **Pennsylvania Dutch Convention & Visitors Bureau** (717/299-8901, www.padutchcountry.com) is an excellent source of information about Lancaster County. Visit the website to request a free "getaway guide" or flip through a digital version. At the CVB's main visitors center (501 Greenfield Rd., Lancaster, 9am-5pm Mon.-Sat. and 10am-4pm Sun. Memorial Day weekend-Oct., 10am-4pm

daily Nov.-Memorial Day weekend), located just off Route 30 at the Greenfield Road exit, you can watch a brief film, load up on maps and brochures, and chat with travel consultants. Ninety-minute tours of the Amish countryside depart from the visitors center from Memorial Day through October. The CVB also operates a visitors center in downtown Lancaster (5 W. King St., 717/735-0823, open Tues. and Fri.-Sun. Jan.-Mar., daily Apr.-Dec., hours vary by season).

GETTING THERE AND AROUND

The city of Lancaster is about 70 miles west of Philadelphia via Route 30 and 80 miles northeast of Baltimore via I-83 north and Route 30 east. The Pennsylvania Turnpike (I-76) passes through the northern part of Lancaster County, but many of the main attractions lie along or near Route 30, which traverses the central part.

Lancaster Airport (LNS, 717/569-1221, www.lancasterairport.com) is served by just one airline, Sun Air International. The larger **Harrisburg International Airport** (MDT, 888/235-9442, www.flyhia.com) is about 30 miles from Lancaster city. **Amtrak** (800/872-7245, www.amtrak.com) provides rail service to the city. Lancaster's Amtrak station (53 E. McGovern Ave.), which also serves as an intercity bus terminal, was built in 1929 by the Pennsylvania Railroad. Bus service is available through **Greyhound** (800/231-2222, www.greyhound.com) and its interline partners.

For getting around Lancaster County, it's best to have your own wheels, but public transportation is available. **Red Rose Transit Authority** (717/397-5613, www.redrosetransit.com) operates 17 bus routes throughout the county. It also has a tourist trolley that plies the streets of Lancaster city on weekdays. Trolley stops include the Amtrak station and the Downtown Lancaster Visitors Center.

Reading and Vicinity

With a population of 88,000, Reading is the largest city in Pennsylvania Dutch country. It was laid out in 1748 by sons of Pennsylvania founder William Penn and named the seat of Berks County several years later. By then the area was already home to an Amish community, one of the first in the country. Most Amish left Berks County in the latter part of the 1700s and early 1800s for reasons that may have included their pacifism. Reading was a military base during the French and Indian War, and its ironworks helped supply George Washington's troops with ammunition during the Revolutionary War. After Washington famously crossed the icy Delaware River in December 1776 and captured hundreds of Hessian soldiers garrisoned in Trenton, New Jersey, Reading hosted a prisoner-of-war camp.

The construction of the Reading Railroad in the 19th century ushered in the region's economic heyday. Built in the 1830s and '40s, the original mainline stretched south from the coal-mining town of Pottsville to Reading and then on to Philadelphia, a journey of less than 100 miles. Over the next century, the Reading grew into a many-tentacled transportation system with more than 1,000 miles of track. Heavily invested in Pennsylvania's anthracite coal industry, it reigned as one of the world's most prosperous corporations at the turn of the 20th century. Within a few decades, anthracite coal and rail transportation had both fallen out of favor. The railroad filed for bankruptcy and was absorbed by Conrail in the 1970s. But it lives on in the form of a property in the standard version of the board game Monopoly. One of Berks County's 30-plus historical museums and sites is dedicated to the railroad.

Historical attractions notwithstanding, the county is best known as a shopping destination. It's home to an outlet mall and the only Cabela's outdoor megastore in Pennsylvania. It also has much to offer antiques lovers.

By the way, it's pronounced "RED-ing," not "REED-ing."

SIGHTS
The Pagoda

Reading's most prominent landmark is a building of the sort rarely seen outside the Far East. Perched atop Mount Penn, 886 feet above downtown, the **Pagoda** (Duryea Dr., 610/655-6271, www.readingpagoda.com, noon-4pm Fri.-Sun. in summer and Sat.-Sun. rest of year, suggested donation $1) has become a symbol of the city. You'll see it in the logos of businesses and civic organizations and on a shoulder patch worn by the men and women of the Reading Police Department. More than a century old, it's believed to be one of only three pagodas of its scale in the country and the only one in the world with a fireplace and chimney. The story of how the multitiered tower came to be is as interesting as the structure itself. "Reading to Have Japanese Pagoda," read a headline in the August 10, 1906, issue of the *Reading Eagle*. The man behind the plan was local businessman William Abbott Witman, who had made himself very unpopular by starting a stone quarrying operation on the western slope of Mount Penn. The Pagoda would cover the mess he'd left on the mountainside. Moreover, it would serve as a luxury resort.

The exotic building was completed in 1908, but Witman's plan to operate it as a mountain retreat was dealt a fatal blow: his application for a liquor license was denied. By 1910, the property was in foreclosure. To save the bank from a loss, local merchant and bank director Jonathan Mould purchased the Pagoda and presented it to the city as a gift. Before radios came into common use, the seven-story structure served as a sort of public announcement system. Lights installed on its roof flashed Morse code to direct firemen and relay baseball scores, political outcomes, and

Reading's Pagoda

other information. Today the temple of stone and terra-cotta tiles is a popular tourist stop. Visitors can climb 87 solid oak steps to a lookout offering a view for 30-plus miles. There's a small café and gift shop on the first floor. The Pagoda is quite a sight at night, when it's aglow with red LED lights.

Reading Railroad Heritage Museum

Opened in 2008 in a former Pennsylvania Steel foundry complex, the **Reading Railroad Heritage Museum** (500 S. 3rd St., Hamburg, 610/562-5513, www.readingrailroad.org, 10am-4pm Sat., noon-4pm Sun., admission $5, seniors $4, children 5-12 $3) tells the story of the profound impact the railroad had on the communities it served. It's operated by the Reading Company Technical & Historical Society, which began rounding up locomotives and freight and passenger cars several years after the railroad's 1971 bankruptcy filing. The all-volunteer nonprofit is now the proud owner of the nation's largest collection of rolling stock dedicated to a single railroad.

Reading Public Museum

The **Reading Public Museum** (500 Museum Rd., Reading, 610/371-5850, www.readingpublicmuseum.org, 11am-5pm daily, admission $10, seniors, students, and children 4-17 $6, planetarium show $8, seniors, students, and children 4-17 $6) is part art museum, part natural history museum, and part anthropological museum. Founded in 1904 by a local teacher, the museum even has a gallery devoted to its own history. Its fine art collection is particularly strong in oil paintings and includes works by John Singer Sargent, Edgar Degas, Winslow Homer, N. C. Wyeth, George Bellows, Milton Avery, and Berks County native Keith Haring. Among the highlights of its natural history collection are the fossilized footprints of reptiles that roamed the immediate area some 200 million years ago. They were found just a few miles away. The anthropological and historical collections include everything from an Egyptian mummy to 16th-century samurai armor to Pennsylvania German folk art. As if that weren't enough, the museum boasts a 25-acre arboretum and a full-dome planetarium.

GoggleWorks Center for the Arts

Like other cities wrestling with the erosion of their industrial base, Reading has rolled out

Have a Lager

If Pennsylvania had an official state beer, it would have to be **Yuengling Traditional Lager.** It's so ubiquitous and popular that asking for it by name is oftentimes unnecessary. Most bartenders translate "I'll have a lager" as "Pour me a Yuengling." Pronounced properly (YING-ling), the brand sounds like an import from the Far East. But the brewing company more properly known as D.G. Yuengling & Son has been based in Pottsville, Pennsylvania, since its 1829 founding. Yeah, about its age: Yuengling is America's oldest brewery, a fact stamped on every bottle. It survived Prohibition by producing "near beers"—now known as nonalcoholic beers—and celebrated the 1933 repeal of the 18th Amendment by shipping a truckload of real beer to the White House. We don't know how then-president Franklin Roosevelt felt about the suds, but Barack Obama is a fan. When he lost a friendly wager on the outcome of the U.S.-Canada battle for ice hockey gold at the 2010 Winter Olympics, he sent a case of "lager" (as in Yuengling) to the Canadian prime minister.

About 35 miles north of Reading, Pottsville lies in Pennsylvania's coal region, home to the largest fields of anthracite in the country. The city is still recovering from the demise of the anthracite industry after World War II. Yuengling also had it rough in the post-war decades, as the full-flavored products of regional breweries lost favor to lighter national brands. But the company has more than recovered since Richard L. Yuengling Jr. became its fifth-generation owner in 1985. According to a 2013 report by the Boulder, Colorado-based Brewers Association, Yuengling is the fourth largest brewing company in the country. Only Anheuser-Busch, MillerCoors, and Pabst sell more suds. Its rapid growth has much to do with the popularity of "lager," introduced in 1987. Yuengling produces half a dozen other beers but sells more lager than all the rest combined.

Free tours of the Pottsville **brewery** (5th and Mahantongo Streets, 570/628-4890, www.yuengling. com, gift shop open 9am-4pm Mon.-Fri. year-round and 10am-3pm Sat. Apr.-Dec.) are offered at 10am and 1:30pm weekdays year-round and from 11am to 1pm on Saturdays April-December. They include a visit to the "caves" where beer was fermented in years past, and end with free samples. You don't have to be of drinking age to take a tour, but you do have to wear closed shoes. Built in 1831, the facility isn't handicapped accessible.

While in Pottsville, you may want to pay a visit to **Jerry's Classic Cars and Collectibles Museum** (394 S. Center St., 570/628-2266, www.jerrysmuseum.com, noon-5pm Fri.-Sun. May-Oct., admission $8, seniors $6, children 6 and under free), a tribute to the 1950s and '60s.

the red carpet for artists and cultural organizations. In 2005 an abandoned factory in Reading's urban core was transformed into the **GoggleWorks Center for the Arts** (201 Washington St., Reading, 610/374-4600, www. goggleworks.org, 11am-7pm daily, free admission). So named because the factory manufactured safety goggles, the arts center boasts several galleries, a film theater, a café, dozens of artist studios, a wood shop, a ceramics studio, a jewelry studio, a glassblowing facility, dance and music studios, and more. The best time to visit is on the **second Sunday** of the month, when most of the artists are in their studios. Held 11am-4pm, the open house features live music and walk-in workshops.

The **GoggleWorks Store** (11am-7pm Mon.-Fri., 11am-5pm Sat.-Sun.) offers unique handcrafted items. GoggleWorks is also home to the **Greater Reading Visitors Center** (610/375-4085, www.gogreaterreading.com), where you can load up on maps and brochures.

★ Air Museums

Berks County is home to not one but two museums dedicated to the history of aviation. Both offer thrill-of-a-lifetime rides in antique planes. Larger and older, the **Mid-Atlantic Air Museum (MAAM)** (11 Museum Dr., Reading, 610/372-7333, www.maam.org, 9:30am-4pm daily, admission $8, seniors $6, children 6-12 $3) at Reading Regional Airport is home to more than 60 aircraft built from 1928 to the early 1980s. Among them is a Northrop P-61 Black Widow—one of only four in existence. In January 1945, the night fighter crashed into a mountainside on the South Pacific Island of New Guinea. World War II veteran Eugene "Pappy" Strine and his son established the air museum in 1980 for the purpose of recovering the rare aircraft, which had logged only 10 flight hours before stalling and crashing during a proficiency check. Green-lighted by the Indonesian government in 1984, the recovery project took seven years. Other highlights of the collection include a North American B-25 Mitchell, a World War II bomber that appeared in half a dozen movies before she was donated to the museum in 1981, and a Douglas R4D-6 Skytrain, which delivered supplies and specialist personnel to combat zones during the war. MAAM's impressive holding of vintage military aircraft and annual **World War II Weekend** have given it a reputation as a "warbird" museum, but in fact, about two-thirds of its flying machines were built for civilians.

Reading's airport was used as a military training airfield during World War II, and for three days each summer, it takes on the look and feel of that era. Held the first full weekend in June, WWII Weekend features air and military vehicle shows, battle re-creations, troop encampments, a militaria flea market, and 1940s entertainment, including big band dances.

The **Golden Age Air Museum** (Grimes Airfield, 371 Airport Rd., Bethel, 717/933-9566, www.goldenageair.org, 10am-4pm Sat. and 11am-4pm Sun. May-Oct., self-guided tour $5, children 6-12 $3, guided tour $8, children 6-12 $3), about 20 miles away, was established in 1997. True to its name, it concentrates on the so-called golden age of aviation: the years between the two World Wars. More than 20 of its 30-some aircraft were built in the late 1910s, '20s, and '30s. The museum is also home to a handful of antique automobiles, including a 1930 Ford Model A roadster. Its **"Flying Circus" air shows,** held twice yearly, pay tribute to barnstorming, a popular form of entertainment in the 1920s.

MAAM offers rides in a pair of 1940s aircraft, including an open-cockpit biplane trainer, on the second weekend of May and July-October, as well as during the WWII extravaganza. The cost of the flight, which lasts about 20-25 minutes, is $225. Reservations are required. Golden Age Air Museum offers rides in an open-cockpit 1929 biplane year-round by appointment. A 15-minute flight costs $99 for one person, $119 for two. One or

World War II reenactment at the Mid-Atlantic Air Museum

two people can fly for 30 minutes for $199 or 60 minutes for $379.

Hopewell Furnace National Historic Site

If you ask Pennsylvanians about the state's iron and steel heritage, they'll probably tell you about the fire-breathing plants that brought renown to cities such as Pittsburgh, Johnstown, and Bethlehem. Most people don't associate the industry with rural Pennsylvania. They haven't been to **Hopewell Furnace National Historic Site** (2 Mark Bird Ln., Elverson, 610/582-8773, www.nps. gov/hofu, 9am-5pm daily in summer and Wed.-Sun. in other seasons, free admission), which features the restored remains of an iron furnace and the village that grew around it. Established in 1771, Hopewell Furnace was one of dozens of "iron plantations" operating in southeastern Pennsylvania by the time the American colonies declared their independence from Great Britain. It supplied cannons, shot, and shells for patriot troops during the Revolutionary War. During the first half of the 19th century, the charcoal-fired furnace produced a wide variety of iron products, including pots, kettles, flatirons, and hammers, gaining fame for its stoves. Even Joseph Bonaparte, elder brother of Napoleon, ordered a Hopewell stove in 1822. After 112 years of operation, the outdated furnace closed in 1883. The workers and their families packed up and left.

Purchased by the federal government in 1935, the Hopewell Furnace property has been restored to the way it looked during its heyday in the 1830s and '40s. Visitors still have to use their imaginations: The National Park Service lacks the wizardry to re-create the billows of charcoal dust, noises, and stench that emanated from the active furnace. Exhibits in the visitors center and occasional living history programs help the imagination. The core of the Hopewell Furnace experience is strolling through the frozen-in-time village, popping into open buildings, so it's best to visit when the weather is nice. Early September through October is a particularly good time because the park's apple orchard, which includes historic varieties you won't find in the supermarket, is open for picking. The apples are sold by the pound. Hiking enthusiasts should plan to stay a while. More than 40 miles of trails traverse the 848-acre historic site and neighboring **French Creek State Park** (843 Park Rd., Elverson, 610/582-9680, www.visitpaparks.com).

Roadside America

Billed as "the world's greatest indoor miniature village," **Roadside America** (109 Roadside Dr., Shartlesville, 610/488-6241, www.roadsideamericainc.com, 9am-6:30pm weekdays and 9am-7pm weekends July-Labor Day, 10am-5pm weekdays and 10am-6pm weekends Sept.-June, admission $6.75, children 6-11 $3.75) ranks among the most unique attractions in Pennsylvania. The massive display features more than 300 miniature structures, 4,000 miniature people, and 10,000 miniature trees. There are horse-drawn carriages and muscle cars, trolleys and trains, construction crews and a coal mine. There's even an animated circus. Started in the 1930s by a local carpenter, the masterpiece depicts rural life from pioneer days to the present. In addition to Roadside America, the small town of Shartlesville offers Pennsylvania Dutch food and quaint shops. It's in northern Berks County, about 20 miles northwest of Reading.

★ Hawk Mountain Sanctuary

Located 25 miles north of Reading, **Hawk Mountain Sanctuary** (1700 Hawk Mountain Rd., Kempton, 610/756-6000, www.hawkmountain.org, trails open dawn to dusk daily except during deer season in Dec., visitors center open 8am-5pm daily Sept.-Nov., 9am-5pm Dec.-Aug.) is one of the best places in the country to watch migrating hawks, eagles, falcons, and other winged predators. During the fall migration, counters may record upwards of 1,000 birds in one day. That's because of the sanctuary's location on the Blue Mountain (aka Kittatinny) ridge, part of the

Appalachian range. In the fall, the topography and prevailing northwesterly winds conspire to create updrafts that allow raptors to glide, soar, and save energy on their southward journeys. Lookouts at Hawk Mountain allow for eye-level views of the majestic birds. Some fly so close that you can't help but duck. The migration begins in mid-August and continues into December, peaking September through November. The very best time to visit is two or three days after a cold front passes. Sightings are considerably less frequent during the northbound migration, when prevailing easterlies push raptors west of the sanctuary. Still, it's possible to spot as many as 300 on a day in April or early May.

Founded in 1934 to stop hunters from shooting the migrants, Hawk Mountain is the world's oldest refuge for birds of prey. The nonprofit charges a fee for use of its eight-mile trail system, which connects to the epic Appalachian Trail. The fee is $6 for adults, $5 for seniors, and $3 for children 6-12 except on national holidays and autumn weekends, when adults and seniors pay $8 and children $4. The most popular path winds past a series of lookouts and is known, appropriately enough, as the Lookout Trail. The first

lookout is only a couple hundred yards from the trailhead and is accessible by all-terrain wheelchair, available at the visitors center. The trail becomes rocky and uneven after the first few overlooks, but soldier on and you'll reap just rewards. At the end of the mile-long trail is the famed **North Lookout,** site of the sanctuary's official hawk count. It's hard to tear yourself away from the panoramic view from 1,490 feet above sea level, so consider bringing a cushion and something to eat or drink. Definitely pack food and water if you plan to tackle longer trails like the four-mile River of Rocks loop, which drops into a valley and skirts an ice-age boulder field. Trail maps are available on the sanctuary's website and in the visitors center.

If you're new to bird-watching, browse the visitors center's educational displays before starting your hike. A bit of time in the Wings of Wonder Gallery, featuring life-size wood carvings of each migrating raptor, will do wonders for your ability to identify the real deal. You'll more than likely meet longtime visitors as you explore the sanctuary, many of whom can chirp up a storm about spotting and identifying birds. Educators are stationed at some lookouts during busy periods.

North Lookout at Hawk Mountain Sanctuary

Hawk Mountain Line

Known as the Hawk Mountain Line because of its proximity to the bird sanctuary, the **Wanamaker, Kempton & Southern** (home station 42 Community Center Dr., Kempton, 610/756-6469, www.kemptontrain.com, regular ticket $10, children 3-11 $5) is a tourist railroad consisting of several miles of track purchased from the Reading Railroad in the 1960s and a collection of rolling stock that includes both steam and diesel-electric locomotives. The Reading began pulling up tracks in the 1970s, leaving the WK&S with two dead ends. Regular and themed train rides are offered on weekends March-December.

The home station is off Route 737 in Kempton, an itty-bitty community about 30 miles north of Reading. From I-78, take exit 35 for Route 143 north or exit 40 for Route 737 north and continue about five miles to Kempton, where signs point the way to the station. Originally part of the vast Reading Railroad network, the station was moved from the southern tip of Berks County to its present location at the northern tip in 1963.

Crystal Cave Park

Discovered in 1871, **Crystal Cave** (963 Crystal Cave Rd., Kutztown, 610/683-6765, www.crystalcavepa.com, opens at 9am daily Mar.-Nov., closes between 5 and 7pm, tour $12.50, children 4-11 $8.50) is the oldest operating show cave in Pennsylvania. Guides who know their stalagmites from their stalactites lead visitors along concrete pathways, pointing out the "prairie dogs," the "totem pole," the "ear of corn," and other exquisite formations. Tours last 40-50 minutes and include a short video presentation on cave geology. It's a constant 54 degrees inside, so dress accordingly.

There's quite a bit to keep visitors entertained outside the cave, including an 18-hole miniature golf course ($4.50), a panning-for-gemstones attraction, and an ice cream parlor and restaurant open daily in July and August and weekends in June and September. Amish buggy rides and use of

the picnic facilities are included in the price of admission.

ENTERTAINMENT AND EVENTS

Concert Venues

Home to Reading's professional ice hockey, indoor soccer, and indoor football teams, the **Santander Arena** (700 Penn St., Reading, 610/898-7469, tickets 800/745-3000, www.santander-arena.com) also hosts concerts, professional wrestling, conventions, and other events. Previous performers include Neil Diamond, Kenny Chesney, Cher, Elton John, and Sting. Opened in 2001, the arena seats 7,200 for hockey and 8,800 for concerts. It's sometimes converted into a smaller, more intimate venue known as the **Reading Eagle Theater.**

Performing Arts

In 2000 the Berks County Convention Center Authority purchased Reading's only surviving movie palace and sank $7 million into renovations. Now known as the **Santander Performing Arts Center** (136 N. 6th St., Reading, 610/898-7469, www.santander-arena.com), the 1,700-seat theater is home to the **Reading Symphony Orchestra** (www.readingsymphony.org). It also hosts touring Broadway productions, popular music concerts, and other events.

The **Miller Center for the Arts** (4 N. 2nd St., Reading, 610/607-6270, www.racc.edu/MillerCenter) also welcomes a wide array of touring acts—from modern dance to classical marionette theater. The glass-walled theater on the campus of Reading Area Community College seats about 500.

Festivals and Events

First held in 1991, **Berks Jazz Fest** (various venues, tickets 800/745-3000, www.berksjazzfest.com, Mar.) has grown bigger and bigger over the years. Famed trumpeter Wynton Marsalis, who played at the inaugural fest, returned in 2010 with his Jazz at Lincoln Center Orchestra. Other past performers include Béla

Fleck and the Flecktones, the Count Basie Orchestra, and Kurt Elling. The 10-day festival is presented by the Berks Arts Council, which is also to thank for a series of free concerts held on Friday evenings in the summer. These **Bandshell Concerts** (City Park, 1261 Hill Rd., Reading, 610/898-1930, www.berksarts.org) showcase various musical genres, including blues, doo-wop, and bluegrass.

Berks County's premier event is the **Kutztown Folk Festival** (Kutztown Fairgrounds, 225 N. White Oak St., Kutztown, 888/674-6136, www.kutztownfestival.com, late June/early July, admission charged, free for children 12 and under), a nine-day celebration of Pennsylvania Dutch culture. Founded in 1950, it's said to be the oldest continuously operated folklife festival in the country. To call it a unique event is an understatement. Where else can you see a reenactment of a 19th-century hanging, watch a Mennonite wedding, take a seminar on the Pennsylvania Dutch dialect, *and* buy bread baked in an early 1800s oven? The festival also features one of the largest quilt sales in the country. More than 2,500 locally handmade quilts are available for purchase; collectors from around the world attend an auction of the prizewinners. Demonstrations of quilting and other traditional crafts are a hallmark of the event. The words *Pennsylvania Dutch* are practically synonymous with *pig-out,* and the Kutztown extravaganza does nothing to dispel that association. All-you-can-eat ham and chicken dinners are a festival tradition, as is roasting a 1,200-pound ox over a bed of coals. The borough of Kutztown is about 20 miles northeast of Reading.

Folks who like it hot descend on an itty-bitty community four miles south of Kutztown for the **Chile Pepper Festival** (William Delong Park, 233 Bowers Rd., Bowers, www.pepperfestival.com, Sept., admission by donation). The two-day event features a jalapeño-eating contest, a salsa contest, and excursions to a local chili pepper field.

Winter's main event is a Christmas display on steroids. **Koziar's Christmas Village** (782 Christmas Village Rd., Bernville, 610/488-1110, www.koziarschristmasvillage. com, first weekend of Nov. to Jan. 1, admission charged) traces its history to 1948, when William M. Koziar strung lights around his house and barn in rural Berks County to the delight of his wife and four children. Each year, he stepped up his game, decorating more and more of his property. The increasingly elaborate display began attracting people from nearby and then people from not-so-nearby. These days more than half a million Christmas lights go into the creation of the winter wonderland. A reflective lake doubles the wow factor. There's more to Koziar's than twinkling lights. It also offers large dioramas of scenes such as "Christmas Beneath the Sea" and "Santa's Post Office," extensive model train layouts, and shops selling ornaments, souvenirs, toys, and other gifts. Santa's on-site, of course.

SHOPPING
VF Outlet Center

One of greater Reading's most popular tourist destinations, the **VF Outlet Center** (801 Hill Ave., Wyomissing, 610/378-0408, www. vfoutletcenter.com, 9:30am-9pm Mon.-Sat., 10am-6pm Sun., call for winter hours) has a rich history. For most of the 20th century, its buildings comprised the Berkshire Knitting Mills. The Berkie, as locals called it, was the world's largest manufacturer of hosiery in the early decades of the century, before seamless nylons became all the rage. In 1969 it was purchased by VF Corporation, which opened a factory store in one end of a manufacturing building. A drop cloth separated the retail and manufacturing areas. The mill ceased operations several years later, but the store remained. Today the VF Outlet store sells brands including Wrangler, Lee, JanSport, and Nautica. Other stores in the mill-turned-mall include Timberland, Reebok, OshKosh B'gosh, and Dooney & Bourke.

Cabela's

The 2003 opening of a **Cabela's** (100 Cabela Dr., Hamburg, 610/929-7000, www.cabelas.

com, 8am-9pm Mon.-Sat., 9am-8pm Sun., call for winter hours) store less than 20 miles north of Reading warranted a story in *The New York Times* travel section. After all, it was the first Cabela's outpost on the East Coast. The revered retailer of outdoor gear has since expanded into Connecticut and Maine, but the Pennsylvania store still reels in millions of hunting and fishing enthusiasts a year. The 250,000-square-foot showplace just off I-78 features shooting and archery ranges, massive aquariums, life-size wildlife dioramas that put many natural history museums to shame, and a restaurant offering sandwiches stuffed with your choice of meats—the choices including elk, wild boar, bison, and ostrich. And then there's the merchandise. The dizzying selection includes everything from guns to outdoor-inspired home decor. Live bait is available for anglers heading to nearby waters. Also available: kennels for shoppers who bring their canine friends, a corral for those who bring their equine friends, and a dump station for those arriving by RV.

Antiques

Antiques lovers can find plenty of what they're looking for in the Reading area. Just 10 miles southwest of Reading, straddling Berks and Lancaster Counties, is the borough of Adamstown, also known as "Antiques Capital USA." See the *Lancaster County* section for the lowdown on Adamstown. Twenty miles northeast of Reading is another antiquing destination: Kutztown's **Renninger's** (740 Noble St., Kutztown, 610/683-6848, www.renningers.com, antiques and flea markets 8am-4pm Sat., farmers market 10am-7pm Fri. and 8am-4pm Sat.). With locations in Adamstown and Florida as well as Kutztown, Renninger's is a big name in antiquing circles. The Kutztown location is open Saturdays and the Adamstown location Sundays, so it's not unusual for treasure hunters to hit both in one weekend. The Kutztown location offers more than antiques; it also boasts a flea market and year-round farmers market. What's for sale? Everything from Indian artifacts and

early farm tools to neon beer signs and Pez dispensers. The farmers market has a strong Pennsylvania Dutch flavor. You'll find produce, fresh and smoked meats, baked goods, handmade candies, gourmet coffees and teas, and french fries to die for.

ACCOMMODATIONS
Reading

Though it's the cultural, governmental, and business capital of Berks County, downtown Reading has few lodging options. Its only hotel is the historic ★ **Abraham Lincoln** (100 N. 5th St., 610/372-3700, www.wyndhamreadinghotel.com, $120-160), a Wyndham property since 2005. Conveniently located within three blocks of the GoggleWorks Center for the Arts, the Santander Arena, and the Santander Performing Arts Center, the recently renovated hotel has 104 guest rooms, two restaurants, a 24-hour gift shop, and free shuttle service to area businesses and attractions. Abraham Lincoln never slept here. The hotel, which opened in 1930, is named for the nation's 16th president because his great-grandfather lived nearby. Music fans and marines will be interested to know that John Philip Sousa, the famed composer of military marches, suffered a heart attack while rehearsing in the area in 1932 and died in his 14th-floor room at the Abraham Lincoln. With its original chandeliers, stately pillars, and brass and wrought iron railings, the hotel lobby is worth a peek even if you're just passing by.

The great stone mansion now known as the **Stirling Guest Hotel** (1120 Centre Ave., 610/373-1522, www.stirlingguesthotel.net, $150-275) was built in the early 1890s in what was then considered a far suburb of Reading. It's a mere mile north of the city center. Designed in the Châteauesque style for a local iron and steel magnate and named for a castle in Scotland, the mansion has nine sumptuously decorated guest suites. A large Tudor-style carriage house offers six more.

Less than a mile north of the VF Outlet Center, **The Inn at Reading** (1040 N. Park

Rd., Wyomissing, 610/372-7811, www.inna-treading.com, $100-150) has 170 tradition-ally furnished rooms and suites. Amenities include a large outdoor pool open May-September, a half-court basketball court, an exercise facility, and a restaurant modeled on a traditional English pub. Breakfast is on the house Monday-Friday.

Northern Berks County

Pheasants, quail, and chukar, oh my! **Wing Pointe** (1414 Moselem Springs Rd., Hamburg, 610/562-6962, www.wingpt.com) is a resort custom-made for sport-shooting enthusiasts. From September through March, shotgun-toting guests hunt game birds released onto the grounds. Rental dogs and guides are available. The resort, 15 minutes from outdoor me-gastore Cabela's, also offers skeet and sporting clays shooting. Its main lodge features four guest suites ($145-191), a common room with a fireplace and large-screen TV, and an out-door pool and whirlpool. Parties of up to nine people can rent a five-bedroom retreat ($550 for four guests, $83 per additional guest) with plush furnishings, a large modern kitchen, a formal dining room, and its own pool and whirlpool.

For those who venture to these parts to aim binoculars rather than shotguns at birds, there's ★ **Pamela's Forget Me Not B&B** (33 Hawk Mountain Rd., Kempton, 610/756-3398, www.pamelasforgetmenot.com, $115-170). A short drive from the famed Hawk Mountain Sanctuary and the Appalachian Trail, the B&B is as charming as its name. It offers three suites complete with whirlpool tubs and one room with a shared bath. Made for romance, the Cottage Suite features a handcrafted four-poster bed, gas fireplace, and private deck. (The couple that purchased the B&B in 2006 stayed here as guests on the night of their 1999 engage-ment.) The comfy Carriage House Suite, which sleeps up to six people, is perfect for families. The remaining suite and guest room are in the main house, dating to 1879 and Victorian in decor.

FOOD
Reading

Most of Reading's recommended restau-rants are concentrated in the gritty down-town area. The most famous, thanks to its longevity and a 2008 visit from the Travel Channel, is **Jimmie Kramer's Peanut Bar** (332 Penn St., 610/376-8500, www.peanutbar.com, 11am-11pm Mon.-Thurs., 11am-mid-night Fri., noon-midnight Sat., $7-25). At the "bar food paradise," as the Travel Channel dubbed it, patrons are welcomed with a bowl of peanuts and encouraged to toss the shells on the floor. The casual joint is also known for its hot wings, seafood, house-made des-serts, and draft beer blends. Opened in 1933 as Jimmie Kramer's Olde Central Cafe, the bar and restaurant originally plied patrons with pretzels. When the pretzels ran out one day in 1935, Jimmie sent someone to a peanut roaster across the street, and the shell-tossing tradition was born. Renamed for the humble legume in 1958, the restaurant is now run by Jimmie's grandson.

One block south of the Peanut Bar is a cluster of three eateries owned by local chef Judy Henry. **Judy's on Cherry** (332 Cherry St., 610/374-8511, www.judysoncherry.com, open for lunch Tues.-Fri. and dinner Tues.-Sat., lunch $8-14, dinner $9-30) offers Mediterranean-style fare, most of it cooked in a 6,000-pound hearth-stone oven. The lunch menu features salads, sandwiches, and pasta dishes. Dinnertime selections include the likes of pan-seared golden sea bass and half rack of lamb. Elegant small plates and crispy pizzas are always on offer, and warm focaccia is free with every meal. The adjoining **Speckled Hen Cottage Pub & Alehouse** (30 S. 4th St., 610/685-8511, www.speckledhenpub.com, 4:30pm-midnight Wed.-Sat., $10-23) offers an altogether different dining experience. Henry transformed downtown Reading's oldest building—a log house built in the 1780s—into the sort of pub you'd find in the countryside of England or Ireland. With its working fire-places and comfort cuisine (chicken pot pie, bangers and mashed potatoes, baked mac and cheese, and such), the Speckled Hen hits the spot on a wintry day. On a warm day, make a beeline for **Plein Air** (610/374-8511, open for lunch Tues.-Fri. and dinner Tues.-Sat. mid-May-Sept., $8-18), an outdoor café accessible from either Judy's or the Speckled Hen. The fare is light and summery, and the featured cocktails are delish.

Just outside the downtown area is the lovely **Abigail's Tea Room** (1441 Perkiomen Ave., 610/376-6050, www.abigailstearoom.com, 11am-3pm Wed.-Sat., open Sun. in Dec. with reservation), which offers a simple lunch menu (under $10) as well as high tea experiences ($19-22). For the latter, be sure to make a reservation at least a day in advance. Abigail's is Victorian through and through, from its setting—an 1883 manse outfitted with period furnishings and crystal chandeliers—to its delicate floral china. Lady Gaga has been photographed with exquisite teacups purchased from the owner's website.

In 2012 downtown's chicest dining establishment relocated to a 200-year-old inn a few miles south of town. ★ **Dans at Green Hills** (2444 Morgantown Rd., 610/777-9611, www.dansatgreenhills.com, 4pm-9pm Tues.-Sat., $19-36) is no longer owned by the two Dans who opened it in 1989 but carries on their mission of providing "a contemporary alternative to the traditional Berks County dining scene." If it's fine dining you seek, look no further.

Northern Berks County

With a name like **Deitsch Eck** (87 Penn St., Lenhartsville, 610/562-8520, www.deitscheck.com, 4pm-8pm Wed.-Fri., 11:30am-8pm Sat., 11:30am-7pm Sun., $4-15), it has to be Pennsylvania Dutch. Chef-owner Steve Stetzler began working in the corner restaurant (*Deitsch Eck* means "Dutch Corner") when he was 15 and bought it nine years later in 1997. His mother and sister are among the staff. In addition to heaping portions of Pennsylvania Dutch cooking, they serve a wide variety of burgers and sandwiches and Italian favorites like veal parmigiana. A meat market in their quaint country town provides the ground beef, hams, pork chops, and sausages.

INFORMATION AND SERVICES

The **Greater Reading Convention & Visitors Bureau** (610/375-4085, www.gogreaterreading.com) is a good source of information about the area. Visit the website to request a free copy of its official visitors guide or peruse a digital version. The guide and some 300 brochures are available at the CVB's visitors center in the **GoggleWorks Center for the Arts** (201 Washington St., Reading, 11am-7pm daily).

GETTING THERE AND AROUND

Located about 60 miles northwest of Philadelphia via I-76 west and I-176 north and 30 miles northeast of Lancaster, Reading is primarily a drive-to destination. There's no scheduled service to Reading Regional Airport, home to the Mid-Atlantic Air Museum. **Lehigh Valley International Airport** (ABE, 800/359-5842, www.flyvia.com), served by airlines including Delta and United, is 40 miles from Reading. **Harrisburg International Airport** (MDT, 888/235-9442, www.flyhia.com) and **Philadelphia International Airport** (PHL, 215/937-6937, www.phl.org) are about 60 miles away.

Intercity bus service to Reading is available through **Greyhound** (20 N. 3rd St., 800/231-2222, www.greyhound.com) and its interline partners. Local bus service is provided by the Berks Area Reading Transportation Authority, or **BARTA** (610/921-0601, www.bartabus.com). Call **Reading Metro Taxi** (610/374-5111) if you need a lift.

Hershey and Vicinity

Hershey is a town built on chocolate as surely as if cocoa were used in place of concrete. It owes its name and existence to Milton S. Hershey, founder of the largest chocolate company in North America. Milton Hershey was born in 1857 in a small central Pennsylvania community. His family moved frequently while his father pursued a series of get-rich schemes, and as a consequence, he never advanced past the fourth grade. At 14, he began a four-year apprenticeship with a Lancaster confectioner—and found his calling. But the young candy maker wasn't immediately successful. His first candy business, in Philadelphia, collapsed after six years. In 1883 he opened a candy shop in New York. Again, his venture failed. Penniless, he returned to Lancaster and gave it a third try, making caramels by day and selling them from a pushcart in the evenings. A large order from a British candy importer and a loan from a local bank marked a turning point for the persistent entrepreneur. His Lancaster Caramel Company soon became one of the leading caramel manufacturers in the country, and he became a very rich man.

At the Chicago World's Fair in 1893, Mr. Hershey was transfixed by an exhibit of German chocolate-making equipment. He purchased the machinery and had it installed in the east wing of his caramel factory. The Hershey Chocolate Company was born.

Back then, milk chocolate was a Swiss luxury product. Mr. Hershey was determined to develop a formula for affordable milk chocolate, and by the dawn of the new century, he had succeeded. He sold the Lancaster Caramel Company for $1 million, retaining his chocolate-making machinery, and in 1903 broke ground on a new, larger factory. The site: a cornfield in Derry Township, Pennsylvania, about a mile from his birthplace. It wasn't simply nostalgia that brought him back. Mr. Hershey needed fresh milk for his milk chocolate, and the area was rich in dairy farms. There was a railroad line and turnpike nearby. The absence of housing and other infrastructure for future employees didn't faze him. He was bent on building not only a manufacturing plant but also a model town.

The intersection of two dirt roads a short

the town of Hershey at night

distance from the factory became the center of his town. He named one Chocolate Avenue and the other Cocoa Avenue. A trolley system was up and running even before the factory was completed. As Americans fell in love with his chocolate, homes for workers and executives were built on streets named after cocoa-growing regions: Trinidad, Java, Ceylon, and such. Mr. Hershey saw to it that builders used a variety of designs so that the community wouldn't look like a company town. It wasn't long before his eponymous town had a fire company, barber shop, blacksmith shop, gas station, service garage, and weekly newspaper. He had set aside land for a park, and by 1910 it boasted a band shell, swimming pool, zoo, and bowling alley. Today Hersheypark boasts more than 60 rides and attractions, including a dozen roller coasters. Sales of Hershey's chocolates grew even during the Great Depression, and so did the town. Taking advantage of low-cost materials, the chocolate magnate launched a massive building campaign that employed hundreds of people. Among the town's Depression-era landmarks are the grand Hotel Hershey and Hersheypark Arena, home to the Hershey Bears hockey team (originally named the Hershey B'ars) until 2002 and site of a massive

surprise party on Mr. Hershey's 80th birthday. He died in 1945 at the age of 88.

The Hershey Company, as it's now named, does business all over the world. But the company founded by Milton Hershey is still based in the town built by Milton Hershey—a town with streetlights shaped like Hershey's Kisses. It still makes chocolate there. You can smell it in the air. "The Sweetest Place on Earth," as Hershey is called, attracts several million visitors a year. Factory tours are no longer given, but it's still possible to learn a world about chocolate and the man who brought it to the masses. Start at The Hershey Story, one of the newest attractions, for an excellent overview. Of course, if you have kids in tow, as a great deal of visitors do, they'll probably insist on starting at Hersheypark. Wherever you start, pace yourself. This place is right up there with Disney World in its concentration of attractions.

SIGHTS
★ The Hershey Story

The Hershey Story (63 W. Chocolate Ave., Hershey, 717/534-3439, www.hersheystory. org, hours vary but generally open 9am-5pm daily) opened in 2009, the first new landmark building on Chocolate Avenue in 75 years. It

The Hershey Story

Milton Hershey's Orphan Heirs

The mural *Community Builder* by William Cochran, located in the lobby of The Hershey Story, depicts Milton Hershey as if he were visiting modern-day Hershey to witness the growth of his legacy.

Married for 10 years and unable to have children, Milton Hershey and his wife, Catherine, established a boarding school for orphaned boys in 1909. The Hershey Industrial School, as it was called at the time, had an initial enrollment of 10. Catherine Hershey—"Kitty" to her adoring husband—wouldn't live to see its dramatic expansion. After a long and debilitating muscular illness, she died in 1915. Three years later, Milton Hershey transferred the bulk of his fortune, including his stock in the Hershey Chocolate Company, to the trust created to fund the school. Upon his death in 1945, townspeople streamed into the school's foyer, where his body lay in state. The funeral service was held in the auditorium, with eight boys from the senior class serving as pallbearers.

Renamed the **Milton Hershey School** (www.mhs-pa.org) in 1951, it began enrolling girls in the 1970s. Today more than 1,800 underprivileged children from prekindergarten through 12th grade live and learn on the 9,000-acre campus—at no cost to their families. Milton Hershey's endowment has grown in value to more than $7 billion. The school trust's assets include full ownership of Hershey Entertainment & Resorts, the company behind Hersheypark, ZooAmerica, The Hotel Hershey, the Giant Center, the Hershey Theatre, and other products of Milton Hershey's vision of a town rich in recreational and cultural resources.

delivers exactly what its name promises: the story of the man, the company, and the town named Hershey. The story unfolds on the museum's second floor, where visitors learn about Milton Hershey's childhood and rocky road to success, his chocolate-making innovations and creative promotion strategies, his model town, and his philanthropies. Among the artifacts displayed are a chocolate-mixing machine from the 1920s and a Hershey's

Kisses-wrapping machine, both in working order. Admission to the exhibit area is $10 for adults, $9 for seniors, $7.50 for children 3-12.

The main floor features the Chocolate Lab, where visitors get hands-on experience in chocolate-making. Arrive early if you're interested. Classes can only be booked on the day of, and they fill quickly. They're $10 for adults, $9 for seniors, $7.50 for children 4-12. Children under 4 aren't permitted in the lab.

Combo tickets are available for visitors who want to take in the exhibits and take part in a class: $17.50 for adults, $16.50 for seniors, $14 for children.

Also on the main floor is Café Zooka, named after one of Milton Hershey's early chocolate novelties. You won't find his Chocolate Zooka Sticks on the menu (they were discontinued in 1904), but you will find a variety of sandwiches, salads, pizzas, and desserts. Leave room for the Countries of Origin Chocolate Tasting: six warm drinking chocolates, each representing a different chocolate-growing region, for $9.95.

★ Hersheypark

Even before his chocolate factory was built, Milton Hershey had laid out the plans for a town. He'd set aside 150 acres along Spring Creek for a park where his employees could picnic and paddle the day away. The park opened in the spring of 1907 and soon became a tourist attraction, with excursion trains and trolleys delivering fun-seekers from surrounding communities. Today **Hersheypark** (100 W. Hersheypark Dr., Hershey, 717/534-3900, www.hersheypark.com) lures people from across the state and beyond with more than 60 rides and attractions, including a dozen roller coasters. The historic park spends generously to stay current. Five of the coasters were installed in the 21st century, including Lightning Racer, the first wooden dueling coaster in the United States. Bring bathing suits to enjoy Hersheypark's water attractions, which include Tidal Force, one of the tallest splash-down rides in the world, and a 378,000-gallon wave pool. For those who prefer to stay firmly planted on the earth, Hersheypark offers shopping and a busy schedule of live entertainment.

The park is open daily from Memorial Day weekend through Labor Day and some weekends before and after that period. Gates open at 10am and close between 6pm and 11pm. One-day admission is $57.95 for guests ages 9-54, $36.95 for children 3-8 and adults 55-69,

$23.95 for those 70 and older. Hang on to your ticket stub in case you decide to come back the next day; consecutive-day admission is $35.50. The park also offers special "sunset" rates and flex passes good for admission to the park on any two or three days of the season. Hersheypark tickets are good for same-day admission to ZooAmerica.

The park opens several times outside its regular season. **Springtime in the Park** is a chance to preview what's in store for summer over several days in April. **Hersheypark in the Dark** offers Halloween-themed fun. The park is also open in late November and throughout December for **Hersheypark Christmas Candylane.** Meet Santa's reindeer and take in a light show set to holiday tunes at Hersheypark. Then hop in the car and crank up the heater for **Hershey Sweet Lights,** a drive-through spectacular located a few minutes from the amusement park.

ZooAmerica

In 1905, a couple from Lebanon, Pennsylvania, approached Milton Hershey with an idea. Several years earlier they'd emigrated from Germany, where they'd owned 12 prairie dogs and a bear cub. Alas, their yard in Lebanon couldn't accommodate their brood. They figured Mr. Hershey's proposed park could. **ZooAmerica** (30 Park Ave., Hershey, 717/534-3900, www.zooamerica. com, open year-round, hours vary, admission $10.50, seniors and children 3-8 $8.50, free admission with Hersheypark ticket) traces its history to their meeting with the chocolate magnate. The 11-acre zoo is home to more than 200 animals from five regions of North America. Visitors are never terribly far from the critters but have a rare opportunity to get even closer during behind-the-scenes tours ($45), offered Tuesday, Friday, and Sunday mornings and Wednesday and Saturday evenings. Preregistration is required for the two-hour tours. ZooAmerica is connected to Hersheypark by a walking bridge. It also an entrance on Park Avenue (Route 743).

Hershey's Chocolate World

When The Hershey Company ceased factory tours in the 1970s, it gave the public **Hershey's Chocolate World** (251 Park Blvd., Hershey, 717/534-4900, www.hersheys.com/chocolateworld, open year-round, hours vary). Adjacent to Hersheypark, Chocolate World is part mall, part interactive museum. Its shops sell anything and everything Hershey's, including pillows shaped like packets of Reese's Peanut Butter Cups, Twizzlers-shaped pens, and personalized chocolate bars. A primer on the chocolate-making process is available in the form of a slow-moving amusement ride. Passengers are transported from a tropical rainforest where cocoa beans flourish to a chocolate factory, encountering some singing cows along the way. The ride is free; other Chocolate World attractions have an admission fee. The *Hershey's Great Chocolate Factory Mystery in 4D*, which premiered in May 2013, is $7.95 for adults and $6.95 for children 12 and under. The show features animated characters controlled by professional puppeteers, and audience participation determines its outcome. For $14.95, visitors can create their own candy bar and design the package. Chocolate World also has a chocolate-tasting attraction ($9.95, seniors $9.45, children $6.95).

To fill up on something other than candy, head to the food court for sandwiches, soups, pizzas, and of course desserts. If you buy nothing else during your visit to Chocolate World, buy a chocolate milkshake. Worth every calorie.

Complimentary shuttle service is available between Chocolate World and Hersheypark. You can also hop aboard an old-fashioned trolley car for a fascinating tour of the town with a ham of a conductor. **Hershey Trolley Works** (717/533-3000, www.hersheytrolleyworks.com, fare $12.95, seniors $11.95, children 3-12 $7.95) tours depart Chocolate World daily rain or shine (but not in snow).

Hershey Gardens

When chocolate magnate and philanthropist Milton Hershey was asked to sponsor a national rosarium in Washington DC, he decided to create one in his eponymous town instead. "A nice garden of roses," as he called it, opened to the public in 1937 and within five years had blossomed into a 23-acre horticultural haven. Roses are still the specialty at **Hershey Gardens** (170 Hotel Rd., Hershey, 717/534-3492, www.hersheygardens.org, open daily late Mar.-Oct. and select days Nov.-Dec., hours vary, admission $10, seniors $9, children 3-12 $7.50), located across from The Hotel Hershey. More than 5,000 roses of 275 varieties bloom during the summer months. Springtime is pretty special, too. That's when 45,000 tulips of 100 varieties blanket the Seasonal Display Garden and daffodils light up the Perennial Garden. Bold-colored chrysanthemums steal the show in fall. But what most visitors go gaga over isn't roses or tulips or any flower for that matter. It's the Butterfly House, open late May to mid-September. Visitors can observe the entire life cycle of the ethereal insects. Also popular is the Children's Garden, filled with not only flora but also fun activities.

The Hotel Hershey

The Hotel Hershey (100 Hotel Rd., Hershey, 717/533-2171, www.thehotelhershey.com), a Mediterranean-style product of Milton Hershey's Depression-era building campaign, deserves a spot on your itinerary even if you're not staying there. Grand to begin with, the hotel is grander than ever on the heels of a $67 million renovation and expansion that was completed in 2009. Some amenities are exclusively for guests. But nonguests can still have a field day. For starters, they can sink into a chocolate milk bath at The Spa at The Hotel Hershey (717/520-5888, www.chocolatespa.com), better known by its nickname, the **"Chocolate Spa."** Other chocolate-inspired services include a Swedish massage with chocolate-scented oil and an exfoliating treatment with cocoa bean husks. The spa menu also pays homage to Cuba, where Milton Hershey spent much of his time after his wife's death in 1915, buying and building sugar mills. The Noche Azul Soak, for example, is a 15-minute dip in waters infused with Cuba's national flower. The three-story spa overlooks the hotel's formal gardens and reflecting pools.

The hotel's boutiques welcome the general public. Among them is a swimwear store with a particularly large selection of chocolate-brown pieces and a sweets shop known for its cupcakes. One of the oldest and most distinguished restaurants in central Pennsylvania calls the hotel home. **The Circular** owes its shape to Mr. Hershey, who noticed during his world travels that guests who tipped poorly were often seated in the corners of restaurants. "I don't want any corners," he reportedly said. He also saw to it that the restaurant had no pillars, having noticed that single diners were often seated at tables with obstructed views.

Not interested in spa treatments, shopping, or excellent food? Come to The Hotel Hershey for the view. Situated on a hilltop, it overlooks "The Sweetest Place on Earth."

Antique Auto Museum at Hershey

Home to the Lakeland bus used in the movie *Forrest Gump* and a green Cadillac Seville once owned by actress Betty White, the **Antique Auto Museum at Hershey** (161 Museum Dr., Hershey, 717/566-7100, www. aacamuseum.org, 9am-5pm daily, admission $10, seniors $9, children 4-12 $7) is one of the few attractions in town that have nothing to do with chocolate. An affiliate of the Smithsonian Institution, the museum has more than 150 cars, motorcycles, and buses. As many as 100 are displayed at any given time. You don't have to be an auto enthusiast to appreciate the elaborate dioramas depicting scenes such as a 1940s gas station and 1950s drive-in.

Indian Echo Caverns

Geological forces make for family entertainment at **Indian Echo Caverns** (368 Middletown Rd., Hummelstown, 717/566-8131, www.indianechocaverns.com, 9am-6pm daily Memorial Day-Labor Day, 10am-4pm rest of year, admission $14, seniors $12, children 3-11 $8), located four miles west of Hershey off Route 322. The first visitors to the limestone caverns were likely Susquehannock Indians seeking shelter from inclement weather. The caverns still do a brisk business on rainy days, when Hersheypark holds less than its usual appeal. Guides point out

the Antique Auto Museum at Hershey

spectacular formations and share cavern lore during 45-minute walking tours. It's always a cool 52 degrees inside, so dress accordingly. In summer, allot an extra hour if you're bringing kids. The grounds include a playground, a petting zoo, and Gem Mill Junction, where budding prospectors can search for amethyst, jasper, agate, and other treasures.

Hollywood Casino at Penn National Race Course

Not every attraction in the Hershey area was built with kids in mind. Nine miles north of chocolate central, grown-ups gamble on slots and horses at **Hollywood Casino at Penn National Race Course** (77 Hollywood Blvd., Grantville, 717/469-2211, www.hcpn. com, open 24 hours). Live thoroughbred races, a tradition since 1972, are held Wednesday-Saturday evenings throughout the year. The casino, which opened in 2008, is ding-ding-ding 24/7 with the occasional ka-ching! Dining options include the upscale **Final Cut Steakhouse** (717/469-3090, 5:30pm-10pm Wed.-Fri., 5pm-10pm Sat., 5pm-9pm Sun., $25-42) and a buffet restaurant open for lunch and dinner Wednesday-Sunday.

Cornwall Iron Furnace

Cornwall Iron Furnace (94 Rexmont Rd., Cornwall, 717/272-9711, www.cornwalliron-furnace.org, 9am-5pm Thurs.-Sat., noon-5pm Sun., admission $8, seniors $7, children 3-11 $4) was retired from service more than a century ago, but it still has a job to do: teaching visitors about the fiery infancy of America's metals industry. Charcoal-fueled furnaces dotted the Pennsylvania countryside in the 18th and 19th centuries, but this one is unique in its intactness. Indeed, the blast furnace and related buildings are regarded as one of the best-preserved 19th-century iron-making complexes in the world.

What used to be the charcoal barn is now a visitors center with interpretive exhibits on mining, charcoal-making, and iron-making. Other surviving structures include a blacksmith shop, a building where wagons were built and repaired, and a darling Gothic Revival building that served as a butcher shop for the ironmaster's estate.

The iron ore mine, which continued to operate until 1973, is just south of the furnace site and visible from Boyd Street. The open pit mine was sensationally prolific, yielding more than 100 million tons before beginning to flood. Today it's filled with water. Houses built in the 19th century for miners and furnace workers still line Boyd Street.

ENTERTAINMENT AND EVENTS
Performance Venues

Best known as the home arena of the Hershey Bears hockey team, **Giant Center** (550 W. Hersheypark Dr., Hershey, 717/534-3911, www.giantcenter.com) hosts some of the flashiest performers to pass through Hershey. It opened in 2002 with a Cher concert. More recent guests have included 50 Cent, Kelly Clarkson, the Harlem Globetrotters, and the Ringling Bros. and Barnum & Bailey circus. Less-than-famous folks can hit the ice during occasional public skating sessions. The arena seats 10,000-12,500 depending on the nature of the event.

Hersheypark Stadium (100 W. Hersheypark Dr., Hershey, 717/534-3911, www.hersheyparkstadium.com) can accommodate 30,000 fans for concerts. The outdoor stadium has hosted the likes of The Who and U2. It's also the venue for sporting events such as the Big 33 Football Classic, an annual all-star game between high school players from Pennsylvania and Ohio. Built as part of Milton Hershey's Depression-era building campaign, the stadium at one point served as the summer home of the Philadelphia Eagles. The **Star Pavilion** opened at Hersheypark Stadium in 1996. It's a more intimate open-air venue with reserved and lawn seating for 8,000.

The spectacular **Hershey Theatre** (15 E. Caracas Ave., Hershey, 717/534-3405, www. hersheytheatre.com) went up during Mr. Hershey's "Great Building Campaign," which created jobs for an estimated 600 skilled workers. The lobby boasts a floor laid with polished Italian lava rock, soaring marble arches, and a ceiling adorned with bas-relief images of swans, war chariots, and more. An intricate lighting system creates the illusion of twinkling stars and floating clouds overhead. The 1,904-seat theater hosts touring Broadway shows, concerts, dance performances, and classic films.

For a list of events at Giant Center, Hersheypark Stadium, Star Pavilion, and Hershey Theatre, visit www.hersheyentertainment.com. If you catch a summer concert at any of these venues, you can visit Hersheypark the day before, day of, or day after the concert for a discounted admission price of $38.95. Present your ticket or ticket stub at Hersheypark's front gate to receive the discount.

Festivals and Events

With Hersheypark closed and temps that dip below freezing, February wouldn't seem like a good time to visit Hershey. If you're a bargain-hunting chocolate lover, it's an ideal time. Each day of **Chocolate-Covered February** (800/437-7439, www.chocolate-coveredfebruary.com) brings a host of chocolate-themed activities along with discounts on everything from museum tickets to spa treatments. The month-long celebration of Hershey's signature foodstuff features chocolate-inspired meals, chef demonstrations, and classes in topics such as truffle-making, chocolate martini mixology, and wine and chocolate pairing.

There's no shortage of entertainment in Hershey during the summer months, but fans of classical and jazz music may wish to head east, to Mount Gretna. The resort community about 12 miles from Hershey has long been known as a cultural mecca. It's home to the **Pennsylvania Chautauqua** (general information 717/964-3270, summer programs 717/964-1830, www.pachautauqua.org), which sponsors Thursday evening organ recitals, a Friday morning writers' series, and a host

of other cultural and educational programs throughout the summer. **Music at Gretna** (717/361-1508, www.gretnamusic.org), a classical chamber music and jazz festival spanning several weeks, has welcomed the likes of jazz pianist Dave Brubeck and singer/guitarist John Pizzarelli.

Hershey draws thousands of antique automobile enthusiasts during the first full week of October. The **Antique Automobile Club of America's Eastern Division Fall Meet** (717/566-7720, www.aaca.org), held in Hershey since 1955, is one of the largest antique automobile shows and flea markets in the country.

SHOPPING

The **Tanger Outlets Hershey** (46 Outlet Square, Hershey, 717/520-1236, www.tangeroutlet.com, 9:30am-9pm Mon.-Sat., 11am-5pm Sun.) are just off Hershey Park Drive, within minutes of Hersheypark and other main attractions. Brooks Brothers, J.Crew, Calvin Klein, Tommy Hilfiger, and Polo Ralph Lauren are among the 60-some stores.

SPORTS AND RECREATION
Spectator Sports

The **Hershey Bears** (Giant Center, 550 W. Hersheypark Dr., Hershey, 717/508-2327, www.hersheybears.com) have competed in the professional American Hockey League without interruption since 1938. Amateur hockey came to Hershey even earlier, in 1931. The popularity of matches between college teams convinced chocolate czar Milton S. Hershey and his longtime chief of entertainment to sponsor a permanent team the following year. They called it the Hershey B'ars. Renamed the Hershey Bears in 1936, the team has brought home at least one Calder Cup, the AHL's ultimate prize, every decade since the 1940s. The Bears "draw more fans and inspire more passion than just about any team in minor league hockey," *The Washington Post* wrote of the Washington Capitals affiliate in 2009. Later that year, the Bears became the first team in league history to win 10 championships. They won their 11th Calder Cup in 2010.

ACCOMMODATIONS

Hershey Entertainment & Resorts (800/437-7439, www.hersheypa.com), the company founded when Milton Hershey decided to separate his nonchocolate ventures from the business that made them all possible, controls not only most of the tourist attractions in town but also three lodging properties: the upscale Hotel Hershey, the more affordable Hershey Lodge, and Hersheypark Camping Resort. There are plenty of other places to bed down, but staying at a Hershey Resorts property has its privileges. Guests of The Hotel Hershey and Hershey Lodge get free admission to the Hershey Gardens and The Hershey Story, while campground guests get discounted admission. Other perks include discounted admission to Hersheypark and access to some rides before the gates officially open. Hershey Resorts guests also have the exclusive opportunity to purchase a **Hersheypark Sweet Access Pass** ($209-250, seniors and children 3-8 $125-150), which includes admission to Hersheypark, a meal voucher, various discounts, and best of all, front-of-the-line privileges at most rides.

For obvious reasons, most Hershey hotels charge a heckuva lot more in summer than the rest of the year.

Under $100

Open year-round, **Hersheypark Camping Resort** (1200 Sweet St., Hummelstown, reservations 800/437-7439, direct 717/534-8995, www.hersheyparkcampingresort.com, campsites $36-60, cabins $76-158) offers more than 300 tent and RV sites and cabins ranging from rustic to deluxe. The 55-acre campground is minutes from Hersheypark. Amenities include two swimming pools, a game room, basketball and volleyball courts, horseshoe pits, and a country store. Organized activities add to the fun in summer. Another good budget option: the family-run **Chocolatetown Motel** (1806 E. Chocolate Ave., Hershey, 717/533-2330, www.chocolatetownmotel.com, $54-140), which boasts an outdoor pool. Even during the busiest weeks of the busy season, rates start at just $89.

$100-300

With 665 guest rooms and suites and 100,000 square feet of function space, ★ **Hershey Lodge** (325 University Dr., Hershey, reservations 800/437-7439, direct 717/533-3311, www.hersheylodge.com, summer $260-320, off-season $160-280) is Pennsylvania's largest convention resort. Not surprisingly, it's quite often crawling with convention-goers. But it's also wildly popular with families, won over by amenities including a mini golf course, activities such as poolside movies and family bingo, and appearances by Hershey's product characters. (Who can resist a huggable Hershey's Kiss?) The chocolate theme extends to the decor of the guest rooms, which feature complimentary wireless Internet access, refrigerators, and flat-screen TVs. Guests can catch A&E Biography's *Milton Hershey: The Chocolate King* any time of day.

Hershey has several chain hotels in this price range. Closest to the action: **Days Inn Hershey** (350 W. Chocolate Ave., Hershey, 717/534-2162, www.daysinnhershey.com, summer $190-250, off-season $100-160). Owned and operated by a lifelong Hershey resident, the hotel has more to recommend it than convenience. The rooms are spacious and the staff gracious. Guests get all sorts of freebies: hotel-wide wireless Internet access, a hot breakfast, shuttle service to Hersheypark, 24-hour coffee and tea service, and use of the Gold's Gym less than two miles away. Plus, they get to bring their pets. Another fine choice is **SpringHill Suites Hershey** (115 Museum Dr., Hershey, 717/583-2222, www.springhillsuiteshershey.com, summer $250-260, off-season $125-160), where Internet access and breakfast are likewise free. It's next door to the Antique Auto Museum and freshly renovated. All guest rooms are studio-suites with a pull-out sofa in addition to one or two beds. Both the Days Inn and SpringHill Suites have an indoor pool and whirlpool, a fitness center, and guest laundry facilities.

For homier digs, head to the **1825 Inn Bed & Breakfast** (409 S. Lingle Ave., Palmyra, 717/838-8282, www.1825inn.com, $134-269). The main house has six country-style guest rooms with private baths. A pair of cottages with a more contemporary aesthetic, king-size beds, two-person whirlpool tubs, and private decks seem to have been designed with honeymooners in mind.

Some of the area's most elegant accommodations can be found on a picturesque horse farm. ★ **The Inn at Westwynd Farm** (1620 Sand Beach Rd., Hummelstown, 717/533-6764, www.westwyndfarminn.com, $109-275) is just 10 minutes north of Hershey but, as owners Carolyn and Frank Troxell are fond of saying, "a world apart." Their goal is simple: to pamper the heck out of guests. That means refreshments upon arrival, a bottomless cookie jar, and gourmet breakfasts that reflect the season, often flavored with herbs from their own garden. The Troxells are happy to point guests to good restaurants and even arrange for dinner at the home of an Amish family. Bringing your family? Ask for the carriage house with its full bath, living room, and space enough for six. The main house has nine en suite guest rooms, eight of which have fireplaces, five of which have whirlpool tubs, and all of which have charm in spades.

Over $300

Milton Hershey's plan to build a luxury hotel during the Great Depression met with ridicule. He poured $2 million into the project anyway. When he addressed the first guests of **The Hotel Hershey** (100 Hotel Rd., Hershey, reservations 800/437-7439, direct 717/533-2171, www.thehotelhershey.com, summer traditional room from $400, cottage room from $500, off-season traditional room from $280, cottage room from $380) on May 26, 1933, he also addressed his critics. "When we farmers go to the city, we are impressed by the fine hotels we see there," he said. "So I thought I'd impress the city folks by building a fine hotel on one of our farms. I am of the opinion that there will be a need for this hotel someday, although the prospects do not look very encouraging at the present time." Mr. Hershey's 170-room hotel impressed folks, indeed. Renowned newsman Lowell Thomas, who visited the hotel in its first year, described it as "a palace that out-palaces the palaces of the Maharajahs of India." The Hotel Hershey is even more palatial now, having treated itself to a $67 million facelift and expansion on the occasion of its 75th anniversary. Among the new facilities is an outdoor swimming complex with an infinity-edge pool, whirlpool, and family pool with two large slides. The pool complex also has 14 swanky cabanas complete with flat-screen TVs, ceiling fans, and refrigerators, available to guests for $200 a day. (The hotel has an indoor pool, so guests can still get their swim on during the colder months.) Also added as part of the expansion: 10 luxury guest cottages. Bordering dense woods, the four- and six-bedroom cottages are the hotel's poshest accommodations. Guests can reserve individual bedrooms or an entire cottage. The latter affords them access to a great room with a fireplace, French doors opening to a porch, and other comforts. The hotel's main building has 228 guest rooms and suites, including the especially elegant Milton Hershey Suite with its veranda overlooking the town of Hershey.

FOOD

Some of Hershey's best restaurants are within The Hotel Hershey (100 Hotel Rd., Hershey). Finest of them all is ★ **The Circular** (717/534-8800, www.thecircular.com, breakfast 7am-10:30am daily, lunch noon-2pm Fri.-Sat., brunch noon-2:30pm Sun., dinner 5pm-9:30pm Mon.-Wed., 5pm-10pm Thurs.-Sat., 6pm-9:30pm Sun., breakfast $8-20, dinner $14-49), which dates to the 1930s. Milton Hershey insisted that the restaurant have no pillars or corners, noting that other restaurants seated single diners at tables with obstructed views and poor tippers in corners.

Previously called the Circular Dining Room, the restaurant was redesigned and rebranded in 2013. It's less formal—you can get away with denim—and livelier than its previous incarnation. A large central bar serves up cocktails inspired by the Prohibition era and Milton Hershey's pursuits and travels, several varieties of chocolate martini, and even chocolate-tinged beers. The Circular puts a sophisticated spin on all-you-can-eat dining, offering a daily breakfast buffet ($19.50, children 3-11 $9), a lunch buffet ($23, children $11.50) on Fridays and Saturdays, and a spectacular Sunday brunch buffet ($39.95, children $19.50) complete with seafood bar and carving station. Dinner showcases the restaurant's highly trained servers and ends with a salted caramel, a tribute to Mr. Hershey's first successful candy business. Make a reservation if you're coming for lunch, Sunday brunch, or dinner.

The Hotel Hershey's other restaurants include **Harvest** (717/534-8800, www.thehotelhershey.com, 11:30am-9pm Sun.-Thurs., 11:30am-10pm Fri.-Sat., lunch $12-29, dinner $13-48), which prides itself on using ingredients from nearby farms and purveyors. It's also rightly proud of its burgers and steaks. **Trevi 5** (717/534-8800, www.thehotelhershey.com, 11:30am-10pm daily, lunch $12-21, dinner $12-32), the hotel's newest restaurant, is an Italian grill. Delicious antipastos and meat and cheese platters threaten to sate your appetite before your main course.

Fenicci's of Hershey (102 W. Chocolate Ave., Hershey, 717/533-7159, www.feniccis.com, 11am-1am Mon.-Thurs., 11am-2am Fri.-Sat., noon-1am Sun., $11-27) is spitting distance from Hersheypark, The Hershey Story, and other main attractions, but don't mistake it for a tourist trap. The casual Italian eatery, which dates to 1935, is beloved by generations of locals. It's famous for its upside-down pizza—cheese on bottom, sauce on top—and its homemade meat, marinara, and mushroom sauces. The Italian wedding soup, made daily, is also a hit. The menu is extensive, with several risottos, six parms, and

scores of variations on pasta. There's a kids menu, too. Grown-ups have the benefit of a full bar and late-night hours.

Also popular with locals, **Fire Alley** (1144 Cocoa Ave., Hershey, 717/533-3200, www.firealley.net, noon-10pm Mon.-Thurs., noon-midnight Fri.-Sat., 10am-10pm Sun., bar open until 2am nightly, $8-29) is an offshoot of Harrisburg's Fire House, which occupies a restored 19th-century firehouse. What Fire Alley lacks in historical value it makes up for in style. Inside the suburban eatery, murals, awnings, window boxes, and streetlights create the impression of an urban streetscape, complete with graffiti. Fire Alley's cleverest design element is banquette-styling seating at the bar: all the comfort of a booth with readier access to the bartender. It's the food, of course, that accounts for the large roster of regulars. The kitchen does wings, burgers, veal parmesan—stuff you'd expect from a casual eatery—but also lobster bisque, mussels steamed in Guinness, and seared tuna on seaweed salad. The meatloaf is swaddled in bacon, and the nachos fall in the seafood category. Drop by on a Thursday for $4 margaritas.

The curiously named **What If . . .** (845 E. Chocolate Ave., Hershey, 717/533-5858, www.whatifdining.com, 11am-10pm Mon.-Thurs., 11am-11pm Fri.-Sat., 4pm-10pm Sun., lunch $8-14, dinner $17-33) is in an off-putting location: below street level in the Howard Johnson Inn Hershey. But if you can overlook the lack of natural light, you'll be glad you came. Start with the crab martini and end with the profiterole du jour, made in-house along with every other dessert. In between, tuck into an entrée from the menu of continental cuisine. The extensive wine list is partial to California and the Pacific Northwest.

INFORMATION

The **Hershey Harrisburg Regional Visitors Bureau** (17 S. 2nd St., Harrisburg, 717/231-7788, www.visithersheyharrisburg.org, 9am-5pm Mon.-Fri. and 10am-3pm Sat., also open noon-3pm Sun. May-Oct.) has loads of information about attractions, lodging, and dining in and around Hershey. Visit the bureau's website to request a copy of its annual travel guide or peruse a digital version.

You can also find a lot of useful information on the website of **Hershey Entertainment & Resorts** (800/437-7439, www.hersheypa. com), the company behind Hersheypark, ZooAmerica, The Hotel Hershey, and Hershey Lodge, among other ventures.

GETTING THERE

Hershey is about 30 miles northwest of Lancaster via Routes 283 west and 743 north, and 15 miles east of Harrisburg via Route 322. **Harrisburg International Airport** (MDT,

888/235-9442, www.flyhia.com), about a 20-minute drive from Hershey, is served by several major airlines. Note that while locals refer to the airport as HIA, its Federal Aviation Administration booking code is MDT. That's because of its physical location in the borough of Middletown, about eight miles south of Harrisburg.

Harrisburg is served by **Amtrak** (800/872-7245, www.amtrak.com) and intercity bus companies. Once there, rent a car or hop in a cab to get to Hershey. You can also travel to Hershey from Harrisburg by **Capital Area Transit** (717/238-8304, www.cattransit.com) bus, which stops at Hersheypark and The Hotel Hershey.

Harrisburg and Vicinity

Like many state capitals, Harrisburg isn't much of a vacation destination. It's awfully close to one; Hershey, aka Chocolate Town, USA, is just 15 miles to its east. Most people come to Harrisburg because they have business there, and more often than not, it's government business. That's not to say there's nothing to see or do in the city, which lies on the east bank of the Susquehanna River. Harrisburg has some excellent museums, including the State Museum of Pennsylvania and the National Civil War Museum. It has a charming park along the river and another *on* the river. It has more minor league teams than you can imagine. In recent years the dining and nightlife scenes have improved to such a degree that it's not unusual for innkeepers in the Hershey area to point guests toward Harrisburg for dinner.

The city owes its name to John Harris, who emigrated from England in the late 17th century, built a home on the river near the present juncture of Paxton and Front Streets, and eventually established the first ferry across the Susquehanna. The ferry played an important role in the westward migration of other pioneers and later in the Revolutionary War,

carrying supplies to the Continental army west of the Susquehanna. After the war, John Harris Jr. made plans for a town on his father's land. Harrisburg was incorporated in 1791 and in 1812 replaced Lancaster as the state capital.

Over the next several decades, Harrisburg emerged as a transportation center, first as a linchpin of Pennsylvania's canal system and then as a railroad hub. During the Civil War, the rail yards teemed with Union soldiers. Hundreds of thousands of men received their instructions at Harrisburg's Camp Curtin. With its transportation arteries and trove of supplies, Harrisburg was a target for Confederate General Robert E. Lee. His troops might have captured the vulnerable capital in 1863—they made it as far as Camp Hill, just across the river—had they not received an urgent order to turn south. The Battle of Gettysburg was at hand.

More than a century later, the citizens of Harrisburg would feel threatened once again. In March 1979, the Three Mile Island nuclear power plant, about 15 miles south of the capital, suffered a partial meltdown. Tens of thousands of people fled their homes. The sight of the plant's cooling towers is still somewhat chilling.

It's best to visit Harrisburg during the warmer months, when the Susquehanna calls to boaters and anglers and the riverfront hosts one festival after another. If you have time to venture outside the city, take a trip on the only remaining ferry across the Susquehanna or a hike on the Appalachian Trail.

SIGHTS

Whitaker Center for Science and the Arts

Part science museum, part performing arts center, and part movie theater, the **Whitaker Center** (222 Market St., Harrisburg, 717/214-2787, www.whitakercenter.org, 9:30am-5pm Tues.-Sat., 11:30am-5pm Sun., admission Science Center only $16, children 3-17 $12.50) is downtown Harrisburg's cultural hub. The $53 million center, which opened in 1999, houses the Sunoco Performance Theater and an IMAX theater with an 80-foot-wide screen—the largest in central Pennsylvania. It's also home to the Harsco Science Center, three floors of exhibits about everything from weather systems to the physics of dance. Visitors can venture a hand into a writhing tornado, test their physical and mental fitness,

build bridges, make their own animated video, and more. KidsPlace, a gallery for children five and under, features a miniature version of Harrisburg's Broad Street Market, the oldest continuously operated market house in the United States. Combo tickets for Science Center visitors who want to catch an IMAX documentary are $19.75 for adults and $16.75 for children 3-17. Hollywood movies shown on the giant screen are $13.75 for adults and $11.75 for children.

State Museum of Pennsylvania

Free for more than a century, the **State Museum of Pennsylvania** (300 North St., Harrisburg, 717/787-4980, www.state-museumpa.org, 9am-5pm Wed.-Sat., noon-5pm Sun., admission $5, seniors and children 1-12 $4) implemented an admission fee in 2009, citing "budget considerations." But it's still a bargain. The four-story circular museum next to the State Capitol offers a well-rounded perspective on Pennsylvania's story. The Hall of Paleontology and Geology introduces visitors to earlier life forms, including a massive armored fish that prowled the seas of Pennsylvania and Ohio some 367 million years ago. Also popular is the Hall

a view of Harrisburg

of Mammals, a set of 13 life-size dioramas of native animals in their natural environments. The Civil War gallery features Peter Rothermel's famous painting of Pickett's Charge at the Battle of Gettysburg. Unveiled in 1870, the plus-size masterpiece (32 feet long and almost 17 feet high) toured the country, appearing at the World's Fair in Philadelphia in 1876. Though it garnered much praise, it also came under fire. Critics complained that the dying Union soldiers had angelic countenances while the rebels appeared wracked with guilt.

Access to Curiosity Connection, a play area designed for children ages 1-5, is included in general admission. Planetarium shows are $2 apiece.

Civil War Sights

Though enemy forces failed to reach it, Harrisburg was not untouched by the Civil War. Far from it. The city was a major transportation hub for the North's war effort. Only Baltimore and Washington had more soldiers pass through their railroad stations. It was also a strategic center. Harrisburg's **Camp Curtin,** which opened in April 1861, was the first and largest training facility in the North. Today a statue of then-Governor Andrew G.

Curtin stands in a small park one block north of the intersection of Maclay and North Sixth Streets, where soldiers entered the camp.

At the end of the war, tens of thousands of Union soldiers paraded through the streets of Washington DC toward a reviewing stand in front of the White House. Excluded from the Grand Review of the Armies were the regiments of the U.S. Colored Troops. In November 1865, a parade honoring them was held in Harrisburg. The veterans marched through town to the Front Street home of Simon Cameron, a longtime abolitionist who'd served in the U.S. Senate and, for a spell, as President Abraham Lincoln's secretary of war. He reviewed them from his front porch and delivered a speech in which he promised: "If you continue to conduct yourselves hereafter as you have in this struggle, you will have all the rights you ask for, all the rights that belong to human beings." No other state held such an event. Cameron's residence was donated to the Historical Society of Dauphin County in 1941 and is now known as the **John Harris-Simon Cameron Mansion** (219 S. Front St., Harrisburg, 717/233-3462, www.dauphincountyhistory.org, tours at 1pm, 2pm, and 3pm Mon.-Thurs. and second Sun. of the month, $8, seniors $7, children 6-16 $6). The house

the Whitaker Center for Science and the Arts

has undergone many additions and renovations since it was built in the mid-1700s for John Harris Jr., who founded Harrisburg on land his father had settled. Cameron was responsible for its makeover into an Italianate-style Victorian, adding a grand staircase and solarium and lowering a floor to accommodate a pair of 14-foot-tall pier mirrors he'd found in France. Guided tours reveal what else he snapped up on his way to Russia, where he was sent as U.S. ambassador after his scandal-marred stint as war secretary.

Harrisburg's premier Civil War attraction opened in 2001. The **National Civil War Museum** (1 Lincoln Circle at Reservoir Park, Harrisburg, 717/260-1861, www.nationalcivilwarmuseum.org, 10am-5pm Mon.-Tues. and Thurs.-Sat., 10am-8pm Wed., noon-5pm Sun., admission $10, seniors $9, students $8) bills itself as a bias-free presentation of the Union and Confederate causes, "the only museum in the United States that portrays the entire story of the American Civil War." Its focus isn't on the famous—President Lincoln, General Robert E. Lee, and such—but on the common soldier and the men and women on the home front. Particular attention is paid to the

African American experience. Lifelike mannequins star in depictions of a slave auction, soldier life at Camp Curtin, the amputation of a soldier's leg, and other facts of 19th-century life.

Pennsylvania State Capitol

Completed in 1906, the current **Capitol** (N. 3rd St., between North and Walnut Streets, 800/868-7672, www.pacapitol.com) was the tallest structure between Philadelphia and Pittsburgh for 80 years. It's still among the most ornate. The seat of state power features a spectacular vaulted dome inspired by Michelangelo's design for St. Peter's Basilica in Rome. Architect Joseph Huston incorporated elements of Greek, Roman, Renaissance, and Victorian design into the building, envisioning a "palace of arts." His vision cost a pretty penny, and Huston was sentenced to prison for overcharging the state. There's no charge for guided tours of the Capitol, part of a large complex of government buildings. They're offered every half hour 8:30am-4pm Monday-Friday and at 9am, 11am, 1pm, and 3pm on weekends and most holidays. Reservations are required for groups of 10 or

Pennsylvania State Capitol

more and recommended for smaller parties. A welcome center in the East Wing is open 8:30am-4:30pm weekdays. Its interactive exhibits explain how laws are made.

Other Harrisburg Sights

The **Broad Street Market** (1233 N. 3rd St., Harrisburg, 717/236-7923, 7am-2pm Wed., 7am-5pm Thurs.-Fri., 7am-4pm Sat.) is said to be the oldest continuously operating farmers market in the country. Founded in 1860, it's the sole survivor of six markets that once operated in the city. At its peak in the 1920s, the market just a few blocks north of the State Capitol had more than 725 vendors, many of whom leased space outside and waited years for an indoor stall. Today it has about 40. They hawk everything from hand-rolled soft pretzels to home decor.

One mile north of the Capitol, the **Pennsylvania National Fire Museum** (1820 N. 4th St., Harrisburg, 717/232-8915, www.pnfm.org, 10am-4pm Tues.-Sat., 1pm-4pm Sun., admission $6, seniors and students $5) has fascinating answers to questions you may not have thought to ask. Why were firehouses built with spiral staircases? To keep the horses from climbing them. Why the poles? Because spiral staircases slowed down the firemen. Housed in an 1899 Victorian firehouse, the museum traces the history of firefighting from the days of hand-drawn equipment to modern times.

Lake Tobias Wildlife Park

A little drool never hurt anyone. Bear that in mind as elk, oxen, llamas, and other beasts approach you for a snack at **Lake Tobias Wildlife Park** (760 Tobias Dr., Halifax, 717/362-9126, www.laketobias.com, open daily May-Labor Day and weekends Sept.-Oct., admission $6, safari tour $6, children under 3 free), about 20 miles north of Harrisburg off Route 225. Africa it's not, but the family-owned animal park offers a safari experience that visitors aren't soon to forget. Specially designed safari cruisers—think school buses with their top halves hacked off—ply 150 rolling acres home to some 500 animals. Among them are species rarely seen in these parts, including water buffalo, the ostrich-like rhea, and the zonkey, a zebra-donkey hybrid. The last safari tour departs one hour before closing. Come too late and you can still have a close encounter with residents of the petting zoo, including African pygmy goats, Patagonian cavies, camels, green monkeys, lemurs, and spotted sheep. Not-so-pettable creatures such as lions, tigers, and bears are exhibited in a zoo-like setting.

Millersburg Ferry and Ned Smith Center

Before bridges spanned the Susquehanna River, people and goods crossed it by ferry. John Harris, the first European to permanently settle in the wilderness that would later become Harrisburg, established the first ferry across the river. One survives. Now a nostalgic tourist attraction more than anything else, the **Millersburg Ferry** (717/692-2442, www.millersburgferry.org, operates May-mid-Oct., car $8, walk-on fare $3, round-trip walk-on fare $5) fleet consists of two wooden sternwheelers that accommodate several vehicles as well as about 50 passengers. The ferry service connects the quaint town of Millersburg, about 25 miles north of Harrisburg, to a modern campground (32 Ferry Ln., Liverpool, 717/444-3200, www.ferryboatcampsites.com, campsites $22-47, cabins $45) on the west bank of the river. It's available weekends and holidays in May, daily June through Labor Day, and then weekends and holidays until mid-October. Weekday hours are 11am-5pm, while weekend and holiday hours are 9am-dusk. To reach the Millersburg landing from Harrisburg, take Route 22/322 west to Route 147 north. Follow 147 into Millersburg and turn left onto North Street.

Just outside Millersburg is the **Ned Smith Center for Nature and Art** (176 Water Company Rd., Millersburg, 717/692-3699, www.nedsmithcenter.org, gallery and gift shop 10am-4pm Tues.-Sat. year-round and noon-4pm Sun. Memorial Day-Labor Day, gallery admission $7, seniors and students $2), which celebrates the life and works of a local boy turned nationally recognized wildlife artist. Ned Smith (1919-1985) painted almost 120 covers for the Pennsylvania Game Commission's magazine, created the state's first duck stamp, and illustrated 14 books. Original paintings now command upwards of $60,000. The Ned Smith Center is home to a $1.5 million collection of paintings, drawings, and manuscripts donated by Smith's widow. The center sits on 500 rustic acres crisscrossed by more than 12 miles of hiking, biking, horseback riding, and cross-country skiing trails. The trails are open to the public at no charge.

ENTERTAINMENT AND EVENTS
Performing Arts

The 600-plus-seat **Sunoco Performance Theater** within the Whitaker Center for Science and the Arts (222 Market St., Harrisburg, 717/214-2787, www.whitakercenter.org) hosts live theater, music, and dance by touring and local performers. Resident companies include **Theatre Harrisburg** (717/232-5501, www.theatreharrisburg.com), a community theater that dates to 1926.

Part of the Capitol Complex, **The Forum** (N. 5th and Walnut Streets, Harrisburg, 717/783-9100) is a 1,763-seat concert hall where "star-studded" refers to the architecture as well as some performances. Its ceiling is studded with hundreds of lights of varying levels of brilliance, arranged to depict constellations. Dedicated in 1931, The Forum is home to the **Harrisburg Symphony Orchestra** (717/545-5527, www.harrisburgsymphony.org).

A storm blew the roof off the **Allenberry Playhouse** (1559 Boiling Springs Rd., Boiling Springs, 717/258-3211, www.allenberry.com) during its dedication in 1949. Adhering to the adage that "the show must go on," the theater didn't let a soaked stage get in the way of its 10-week opening season. Today the season lasts more than 40 weeks, starting in March and running through December. The playhouse on the grounds of Allenberry Resort, about 20 miles southwest of Harrisburg, stages musicals, comedies, and dramas with professional actors. Alumni include John Travolta, who sang and danced on the Allenberry stage in 1971, and Norman Fell, best known for his role as Mr. Roper on *Three's Company*.

Festivals and Events

Harrisburg kicks off each year with the largest indoor agricultural event in the nation, the **Pennsylvania Farm Show** (717/787-2905 during show, www.farmshow.state.pa.us, Jan., free). Some 6,000 animals and hundreds of thousands of people pass through the **Pennsylvania Farm Show Complex & Expo Center** (N. Cameron and Maclay Streets, Harrisburg, 717/787-5373, www.pafarmshowcomplex.com) during the weeklong event. Farmers from across the state show off the fruits of their labors—everything from pecans to powerful Percherons—in the hopes of taking home prize money and bragging rights. Come for an education in the state's number one industry, and come on an empty stomach. The Farm Show's best feature could very well be its food court, where a baked potato isn't a humdrum side but a tour de force. Food purchases feed the coffers of nonprofit commodity associations like Pennsylvania Co-Operative Potato Growers Inc. and the Pennsylvania Maple Syrup Producers Council. Though admission to the Farm Show is free, parking is $10.

Harrisburg's largest arts event, **The Patriot-News Artsfest** (717/238-1887, www.jumpstreet.org), brings artists and craftspeople from around the country to Harrisburg's Riverfront Park over Memorial Day weekend. The free festival has been named one of the top 100 arts events in the country by *Sunshine Artist* magazine.

Riverfront Park also provides the setting for the city's annual Independence Day and Labor Day celebrations. Previously known as the Harrisburg Jazz and Multicultural Festival, the multiday **Fourth of July Celebration** (717/255-3020, www.

Carlisle: Car Show Capital

If you love cars, you'll love Carlisle. The Cumberland County seat, about 20 miles southwest of Harrisburg, is named for a town in England, and locals usually emphasize its second syllable. But auto aficionados can't be blamed for thinking the "car" in "Carlisle" has something to do with engines and chrome. The town is the site of collector car, truck, and motorcycle events every season but winter.

Carlisle Events (1000 Bryn Mawr Rd., Carlisle, 717/243-7855, www.carlisleevents.com) rented the Carlisle Fairgrounds when it began producing car shows in the mid-1970s. By 1981 the gatherings had grown so popular that the company purchased the property. Today it produces more than a dozen annual events. Held in April, **Spring Carlisle** is the kickoff to the season and one of the largest automotive swap meets in the world. **Fall Carlisle,** which caps the season, is another opportunity to buy, sell, and celebrate all things automotive. Between them are specialty shows for Corvettes, Fords, GMs, Chryslers, trucks, imports, and tricked-out "performance and style" vehicles.

Car enthusiasts have even more reasons to love Cumberland County. Mechanicsburg, 10 miles east of Carlisle, is home to the **Rolls-Royce Foundation** (189 Hempt Rd., Mechanicsburg, 717/795-9400, www.rollsroycefoundation.org), which operates a research library and museum dedicated to Rolls-Royces and Bentleys. It's open to the public 10am-4pm Monday-Friday. Mechanicsburg—named for the mechanics of an earlier vehicle make, the Conestoga wagon—also has an automobile racetrack that dates to 1939. Motorsports legends including Ted Horn, A. J. Foyt, and Mario Andretti have raced at the **Williams Grove Speedway** (1 Speedway Dr., Mechanicsburg, 717/697-5000, www.williamsgrove.com). The half-mile track hosts weekly sprint car races March-October. Two other racetracks are within a half-hour drive: the **Quarter Aces Drag-O-Way** (1107 Petersburg Rd., Boiling Springs, 717/258-6287, www.quarteracesdragway.com) and the **Shippensburg Speedway** (178 Walnut Bottom Rd., Shippensburg, 717/532-8581, www.shippensburgspeedway.com).

harrisburgrec.com, free) still features a whole lot of music. There's also a lot to keep kids occupied, including amusement rides and video karaoke. **Kipona** (717/255-3020, www.harrisburgrec.com, free), held over Labor Day weekend, pays homage to the Susquehanna River. (*Kipona* means "bright, sparkling water" in the Delaware Indian tongue.) It's a blockbuster of a festival. You've got live entertainment on multiple stages, children's activities, fireworks, food, and more food. You've also got a chili cook-off—not just any chili cook-off but the Pennsylvania State Chili Cook-Off (www.chiefchili.com), a qualifying event for the International Chili Society's world championship. The perennial festival is also the occasion for a Native American encampment on City Island. The powwow, as it's called, features demonstrations of traditional dance, drumming, and arts and crafts. Some 150 artists and craftspeople from around the country sell their works at the southern end of Riverfront Park.

SPORTS AND RECREATION
City Island

Harrisburg's recreational hub is **City Island,** a mile-long island on the Susquehanna River. It's home to the city's minor league baseball team (717/231-4444, www.senatorsbaseball.com) and USL Pro soccer team (717/441-4625, www.cityislanders.com). Spectator sports aren't the half of it. The island boasts a beach, sand volleyball courts, **batting cages** (717/461-3223, www.cityislandfun.com), and an elaborate 18-hole **miniature golf course** (717/232-8533, www.watergolfcityisland.com). It also has several marinas. If you don't have a boat of your own, board the *Pride of the Susquehanna* (717/234-6500, www.harrisburgriverboat.com), an old-fashioned paddlewheeler that plies the river May-November. Alternatively, set off in a kayak or canoe from **Susquehanna Outfitters** (717/503-0066, www.susquehannaoutfitters.com), which also rents bicycles. Other City Island amenities

A Major Minor League Market

The Hershey-Harrisburg region doesn't have a single major league franchise, but its sports fans have plenty to cheer about. *SportsBusiness Journal* named it the top minor league market in the country in 2009 and again in 2011.

Best known of Harrisburg's franchises is the **Harrisburg Senators** (Metro Bank Park, City Island, Harrisburg, 717/231-4444, www.senatorsbaseball.com), the Class AA affiliate of the Washington Nationals. Formed in 1987, the baseball team won the Eastern League championship in its first season. It captured four consecutive championships from 1996 to 1999, becoming the first team in league history to do so. More than 200 of its players have been called up to the majors.

Hockey fans get their fix at **Hershey Bears** (Giant Center, 550 W. Hersheypark Dr., Hershey, 717/508-2327, www.hersheybears.com) games. Originally named the Hershey B'ars, the team has competed in the professional American Hockey League without interruption since 1938. The Bears "draw more fans and inspire more passion than just about any team in minor league hockey," *The Washington Post* wrote of the Washington Capitals affiliate in 2009. In 2010 the Bears became the first team in league history to win 11 championships.

The Bears share Giant Center with the **Harrisburg Stampede** (Giant Center, 550 W. Hersheypark Dr., Hershey, 717/534-3911, www.harrisburgstampede.com), who captured the American Indoor Football championship in 2013. The team moved to the Professional Indoor Football League shortly thereafter. Other area football teams include the **Central Penn Piranha** (717/385-9649, www.piranhafootball.net), which bills itself as the "winningest team in minor league football history."

The region is also home to **Harrisburg City Islanders** (Skyline Sports Complex, City Island, Harrisburg, 717/441-4625, www.cityislanders.com) soccer and **Harrisburg Horizon** (717/298-1083, www.harrisburghorizon.com) basketball.

include a playground, picnic pavilions, an antique carousel, and scaled-down versions of a Civil War-era steam train and San Francisco-style trolley.

You can walk or bike to the island from downtown Harrisburg via the Walnut Street Bridge, which was closed to cars after Hurricane Agnes in 1972. Cars access the island via the Market Street Bridge.

Appalachian Trail

The **Appalachian Trail Conservancy** (www.appalachiantrail.org), the volunteer-based organization charged with managing and protecting the famous footpath, has an information center about 15 miles southwest of Harrisburg. Located right on the A.T., the **Boiling Springs information center** (4 E. 1st St., Boiling Springs, 717/258-5771) is staffed 9am-5pm weekdays year-round. Weekend hours are based on volunteer availability. You can get answers to questions about short jaunts, thru-hikes, and everything in between, plus guidebooks, maps, postcards, and A.T. merchandise.

The A.T. crosses the Susquehanna River at Duncannon, about 15 miles north of the state capital. Duncannon's **Doyle Hotel** (7 N. Market St., 717/834-6789) is a legendary stop along the Georgia-to-Maine trail. It's a bit of a dive, but that's part of its charm. The hotel serves food and drink, accepts mail drops, and plasters its walls with photos of thru-hikers. Rooms are $25 per night.

Boating and Fishing

Almost a mile wide at Harrisburg, the Susquehanna River tempts outdoor lovers to float or fish the day away. Among the enablers: **Susquehanna Outfitters** (City Island, 717/503-0066, www.susquehannaoutfitters.com, open Tues.-Sun. during boating season) with its rental fleet of kayaks, canoes, and stand-up paddleboards. It offers guided floats and shuttle service to points upriver. Experienced paddlers can rent boats by the hour to paddle around City Island or the cluster of islands just upriver.

If you want to paddle for days, fishing in

The *Pride of the Susquehanna* paddles past the Capitol.

secluded coves and sleeping in riverfront campgrounds or primitive island campsites, you want to call **Blue Mountain Outfitters** (Rte. 11/15, 2 miles north of I-81 interchange, Marysville, 717/957-2413, www.bluemountain-outfitters.net, open Tues.-Sun. during boating season, Tues.-Sat. in winter). Located several miles north of Harrisburg on the west side of the Susquehanna, Blue Mountain is a full-service paddle sports store with a wide selection of canoes, kayaks, stand-up paddleboards, and accessories. Rentals are available during the warmer months. Paddlers can start at Blue Mountain and float downstream or hop on a shuttle to explore the river's more northerly stretches. The outfitter, housed in an erstwhile train station, offers lifts to put-ins upwards of 40 miles away for multiday trips. It also facilitates trips on the Juniata River, Sherman Creek, and other nearby waters. Novice paddlers and shutterbugs can leave the piloting to Blue Mountain's pros by booking a trip on the "war canoe"—a 22-foot vessel that can accommodate eight people. The ride is especially thrilling during high water.

The Harrisburg-area section of the Susquehanna is a top-notch smallmouth bass fishery. Anglers can also get bites from catfish, carp, panfish, and other swimmers. Short on poppers, plastic crayfish, or rubber worms? No worries. Harrisburg Mall is home to Pennsylvania's only **Bass Pro Shops** (3501 Paxton St., Harrisburg, 717/565-5200, www. basspro.com, 9am-9pm Mon.-Sat., 10am-6pm Sun.). The mammoth store is as much a spiritual experience as shopping experience for fishing and hunting fanatics. With its 60,000-gallon aquarium and wildlife dioramas, it's also a family attraction. The store boasts a rock-climbing wall, a NASCAR simulator, an archery range, and a boat showroom.

Yellow Breeches Creek, which flows through communities to Harrisburg's southwest and dumps into the Susquehanna three miles south of City Island, is among the most popular trout streams in the state. Anglers interested in the stocking program can visit the **Huntsdale State Fish Hatchery** (195 Lebo Rd., Carlisle, 717/486-3419, www.fish. state.pa.us, visitors center 8am-3:30pm daily), which produces brook trout, brown trout, rainbow trout, and golden rainbow trout, among other species. Fly fishers flock to a mile-long catch-and-release section in the town of Boiling Springs, which has an excellent fly shop, **Yellow Breeches Outfitters**

(2 E. 1st St., Boiling Springs, 717/258-6752, www.yellowbreechesoutfitters.com, open Tues.-Sun.). The shop sells a wide variety of rods, reels, waders, and other gear. It also offers fly-fishing instruction and guided fishing. **Allenberry Resort Inn and Playhouse** (1559 Boiling Springs Rd., Boiling Springs, 717/258-3211, www.allenberry.com), at the downstream end of the no-kill area, offers fly-fishing courses on select weekends.

ACCOMMODATIONS

If you're looking for a central location, look no further than the ★ **Hilton Harrisburg** (1 N. 2nd St., Harrisburg, 717/233-6000, www.hilton.com, $140-250). It's connected by an enclosed walkway to the Whitaker Center for Science and the Arts and a shopping center called Strawberry Square. The State Capitol Complex and City Island are a short walk away. The hotel is at the end of Harrisburg's Restaurant Row, but finding an excellent meal is easier than stepping outside. The Hilton is home to the **The Golden Sheaf** (717/237-6400, www.hiltonharrisburgdining.com, open for lunch Mon.-Fri. and dinner Mon.-Sat., lunch $10-17, dinner $22-48), Harrisburg's only AAA four-diamond restaurant, and **Raspberries** (717/237-6419, www.hiltonharrisburgdining.com, open for breakfast daily, lunch Mon.-Fri., brunch Sun., and dinner Mon.-Sat., $10-26), famous for its Sunday jazz brunch. The hotel's 300-plus guest rooms feature flat-screen TVs, refrigerators, Hilton's trademark Serenity beds, and free wireless Internet access.

Nestled on the west shore of the Susquehanna River, **Bridgeview Bed & Breakfast** (810 S. Main St., Marysville, 717/957-2438, www.bridgeviewbnb.com, $90-120) doesn't have antique furnishings, luxury linens, heaven-scented bath products, or even in-room televisions. Breakfast isn't what you'd call gourmet. It does have killer views of the river and the Rockville Bridge, famous for being the world's longest stone masonry arch railroad bridge. Built in the opening years of the 20th century by the Pennsylvania Railroad, the bridge still sees a good deal of train traffic—which makes the Bridgeview a magnet for train buffs. Formerly a sporting goods and tackle shop, the B&B has 10 en suite guest rooms, each named for a Pennsylvania river.

FOOD

Politicos don't have to venture far from the Capitol Complex to strategize or negotiate over a meal that receives bipartisan approval. Second Street in downtown Harrisburg has such a high concentration of restaurants and bars that it's known as Restaurant Row. Consider taking a walkabout before settling on a choice. One you won't regret: ★ **Café Fresco** (215 N. 2nd St., Harrisburg, 717/236-2599, www.cafefresco.com, 6:30am-11pm Mon.-Wed., 6:30am-1am Thurs.-Fri., 11am-1am Sat., breakfast and lunch under $10, dinner $10-36). By day, it's a chic but casual spot, offering pizza, burgers, sandwiches, and wraps. It glams up in the evening, becoming a destination for swishy cocktails and Asian-influenced cuisine, though casual fare such as pizzas and a Kobe burger are still on offer. After dinner, you can sashay upstairs to get your groove on. At **Level 2** (717/236-6600, www.level2.us, 8pm-2am Thurs.-Sat.), the dress code is "fashionable and fierce," and the DJs are tireless. Bottle service is available.

One of the newest additions to Restaurant Row, **The Federal Taphouse** (234 N. 2nd St., Harrisburg, 717/525-8077, www.federaltaphousehbg.com, 11:30am-2am Mon.-Fri., 11am-2am Sat., 10:30am-2am Sun., $9-28) boasts 100 craft beers on tap and a coal-fired oven. Customers nosh on fire-roasted olives and smoked pork belly while waiting for pork ribs, sausages, chicken skewers, and other hearty fare. The Taphouse also has a wood-fired oven that turns out crispy pizzas with toppings both common and exotic.

Ethnic options on Restaurant Row include **Miyako** (227 N. 2nd St., Harrisburg, 717/234-3250, www.pasushi.net, 11am-10pm Mon.-Thurs., 11am-11pm Fri., noon-11pm

Sat., $5-19), a sushi restaurant that also offers a variety of teriyaki, tempura, and hibachi dishes.

Not every noteworthy restaurant has a 2nd Street address. Third Street is home to the *muy excelente* **El Sol Mexican Restaurant** (18 S. 3rd St., Harrisburg, 717/901-5050, www. elsolmexicanrestaurant.net, 11am-10pm Mon.-Thurs., 11am-11pm Fri., 4pm-11pm Sat., 10am-3pm Sun., $8-23). Owners Juan and Lisa Garcia—he of the Guadalajara region of Mexico, she of Harrisburg—specialize in dishes from his home state, but they pull off burritos, fajitas, and other familiar fare with equal aplomb.

Across the street at ★ **Bricco** (31 S. 3rd St., Harrisburg, 717/724-0222, www.briccopa.com, lunch 11:30am-2:30pm Mon.-Fri., dinner 5:30pm-10pm Mon.-Sat. and 4:30pm-10pm Sun., lunch $11-19, dinner $14-36), chef Jason Viscount creates masterly Mediterranean dishes with the help of students from the Olewine School of Culinary Arts at Harrisburg Area Community College. Though inspired by Tuscan cuisine, Bricco sources Pennsylvania products whenever possible. Particularly popular are its raw-bar offerings and pizzas, baked in a stone oven and topped with delicacies such as fig jam, white truffle oil, and local feta. The restaurant boasts an extensive wine list and a daily changing menu of artisan cheese.

For barbecue connoisseurs, it doesn't get better than **MoMo's BBQ & Grill** (307 Market St., 717/230-1030, www.momosbbqandgrill. com, 11am-10pm Mon.-Thurs., 11am-11pm Fri.-Sat., 11am-9pm Sun., $7-22). Owner Mike Moran has won awards at barbecue battles around the country and created more than a dozen sauces. The mayo-based Alabama White is his personal favorite.

INFORMATION

The **Hershey Harrisburg Regional Visitors Bureau** (17 S. 2nd St., Harrisburg, 717/231-7788, www.visithersheyharrisburg. org, 9am-5pm Mon.-Fri. and 10am-3pm Sat., also open noon-3pm Sun. May-Oct.) is a good source of information about attractions, lodging, and dining in and around the state capital. Visit the bureau's website to request a copy of its current visitors guide or peruse a digital version.

GETTING THERE AND AROUND

Harrisburg is about 15 miles west of Hershey via Route 322 and 40 miles northwest of Lancaster via Route 283. **Harrisburg International Airport** (MDT, 888/235-9442, www.flyhia.com) is served by several major airlines. Note that while locals refer to the airport as HIA, its Federal Aviation Administration booking code is MDT. That's because of its physical location in the borough of Middletown, about eight miles south of Harrisburg.

Amtrak (800/872-7245, www.amtrak. com) provides rail service to the Harrisburg Transportation Center, located at 4th and Chestnut Streets. **Greyhound** (800/231-2222, www.greyhound.com) and other intercity bus operators also deliver travelers to the station.

Local bus service is provided by **Capital Area Transit** (717/238-8304, www.cattransit.com), or CAT. The base fare is $1.75. Call **Keystone Cab** (717/234-4400) for door-to-door service.

DUTCH COUNTRY
HARRISBURG AND VICINITY

York County

Just west of Lancaster County, York County touts itself as the "Factory Tour Capital of the World." Indeed, more than 20 factories open their doors to visitors. Frugal families can live it up here; admission is free in almost every case. So many of the factories are dedicated to guilty pleasures that York County also claims the title of "Snack Food Capital of the World." I know what you're thinking: York Peppermint Patties. Alas, the brand born here in 1940 now belongs to Hershey Co., and the minty, chocolaty confections are made elsewhere. The biggest name on the factory circuit has nothing to do with mmmm-mmmm and everything to do with vroom-vroom. York's Harley-Davidson factory attracts bikers from across the United States and countries as far-flung as Turkey, China, and Australia.

Long before the county became the Factory Tour Capital, its only city, also named York, served as the capital of what would soon be known as the United States of America. The Continental Congress, that body of delegates who spoke for the colonies during the Revolutionary period, met in York for nine months in 1777 and 1778, adopting the Articles of Confederation. The York County Heritage Trust operates several museums and historic sites that offer a window into the past. Murals throughout downtown York also serve as a record of local history.

The county's greatest asset could be its location in the center of Pennsylvania Dutch country. Gettysburg and its Civil War battlefield are 30 miles west of York. Lancaster's Amish farmlands are about that distance to its east. The state capital, Harrisburg, is 25 miles north of the city, and Hershey, aka "The Sweetest Place on Earth," is just 10 miles farther. That makes York County a good base of operations for travelers who want to take in the more touristy areas without paying touristy lodging prices.

FACTORY TOURS

The "Factory Tour Capital of the World" has more factories than you can visit in a day—or even two. You'll find a comprehensive list at www.yorkpa.org, the website of the York County Convention & Visitors Bureau. Bear in mind that most factories don't offer tours on weekends.

The most famous name on the list is Harley-Davidson. The company has been producing its legendary motorcycles in York since 1973. Free tours of the **Harley-Davidson factory** (1425 Eden Rd., York, 877/883-1450, www.harley-davidson.com/experience, tour center and gift shop open 8am-4pm Mon.-Fri.) begin at regular intervals 9am-2pm Monday-Friday. They offer a limited view of the assembly line and last about an hour. Friday isn't the best day to visit because production may not be scheduled. For $35, you can have a two-hour tour that's more personalized and includes access to some "employee only" areas. The in-depth tour is offered at 9:30am and noon Monday-Thursday. It sells out quickly, so it's a good idea to book tickets by phone or online. Children under 12 aren't allowed on the factory floor, but they're welcome in the tour center, which has exhibits about assembly processes and motorcycles for the straddling.

If you're traveling with kids, put **Perrydell Farm Dairy** (90 Indian Rock Dam Rd., York, 717/741-3485, www.perrydellfarm. com, 7am-9pm Mon.-Sat. and noon-6pm Sun., self-guided tours free) on your itinerary. Depending on when you visit the family-owned farm, you might see cows being milked, calves being fed, or milk being bottled. The oh-so-fresh milk is sold on-site, along with ice cream, locally grown produce, and locally baked goods.

To see why York County bills itself as the "Snack Food Capital of the World," head to the borough of Hanover, 20 miles southwest of York. It's home to several munchies manufacturers. Best known for its pretzels, **Snyder's of Hanover** (1350 York St., Hanover, 800/233-7125 ext. 28592, www. snydersofhanover.com, store open 9am-6pm Mon.-Sat. and noon-5pm Sun.) offers free tours at 10am, 11am, and 1pm Tuesday-Thursday. Reservations are required. Snyder's snacks are sold around the world, so the half-hour tours are an education in large-scale manufacturing. You'll get to see the raw material warehouse, finished goods warehouse, packing room, and oven room. Tours start and end at the factory store, where you'll get a free bag of pretzels and bargains on everything from Old Tyme Pretzels, first made in 1909, to the popular flavored pretzel pieces, introduced some 80 years later.

Hanover is also home to **Utz Quality Foods** (900 High St., Hanover, 800/367-7629, www.utzsnacks.com), where you can watch raw spuds become crunchy chips from an observation gallery. The gallery is open 8am-4pm Monday-Thursday and select Fridays. Though famous for its potato chips—Rachael Ray talked up Utz Kettle Classics on her eponymous TV show—the company also makes pretzels, cheese curls, pork rinds, and more. Its outlet store (861 Carlisle St., Hanover,

8am-7pm Mon.-Sat., 11am-6pm Sun.) is two blocks from the plant.

Far smaller than Snyder's or Utz, **Revonah Pretzels** (507 Baltimore St., Hanover, 717/630-2883, www.revonahpretzel.com) takes its name from the town (Revonah is Hanover spelled backward) and its cues from the past. Pretzels are rolled and twisted by hand, hearth-baked, and slowly hardened in a kiln. Word has it that the Pittsburgh Steelers munch on these when they're on the road. Revonah offers free 20-minute tours 8am-1pm Tuesday-Thursday. Reservations are recommended. Visitors can sample a "greenie," a pretzel that's crunchy on the outside but still warm and soft on the inside.

Be sure to wear comfortable closed-toe shoes when you go factory hopping. Open-toe shoes and heels are prohibited in some areas.

OTHER SIGHTS
Central Market
York's public market house is a can't-miss if you're in town on a Tuesday, Thursday, or Saturday. Built in 1888, **Central Market** (34 W. Philadelphia St., York, 717/848-2243, www. centralmarketyork.com, 6am-2pm Tues., Thurs., and Sat.) is not just a showcase for area farmers but also a hopping lunch spot.

DUTCH COUNTRY
YORK COUNTY

the Harley-Davidson factory

In fact, lunch counters outnumber produce stands by more than three to one. You'll find Greek, Filipino, Malaysian, and Caribbean foods. You'll find fresh-cut fries, homemade fudge, and craft-brewed beer. Busy Bee, run by a classically trained chef, serves inventive soups, salads, and sandwiches. Roburrito's, a popular local burrito joint, joined the vendor ranks in 2009. You can't miss its stand, which resembles a foil-wrapped burrito and serves up venison-stuffed burritos during deer season.

Heritage Sites

The **York County Heritage Trust** (250 E. Market St., 717/848-1587, www.yorkheritage.org, peak-season admission to all sites $15, children 6-18 $7, off-season admission $12, children $5) operates several museums and historic sites within walking distance of each other in downtown York. They include the **Colonial Complex** (157 W. Market St.), a set of four buildings that transport visitors to early York. Built in 1741, the Golden Plough Tavern is the oldest structure in town. Adjacent to it is the General Gates House, named for the Revolutionary War hero who occupied it during York's 1777-1778 tenure as capital of the American colonies. Some members of the Continental Congress were so impressed with General Horatio Gates that they plotted to have him replace General George Washington as commander of the Continental army. The Colonial Complex also features a reconstruction of the courthouse where congressional delegates met during their nine-month stay in York and an 1812 log house. The buildings can only be seen by guided tour. Tours are usually offered at 10am, 11am, 1pm, 2pm, and 3pm Tuesday-Saturday April-December, but call 717/848-1587 to confirm.

Other Heritage Trust sites include the **Agricultural and Industrial Museum** (217 W. Princess St., 10am-4pm Tues.-Sat.), which houses artifacts spanning three centuries. Exhibits cover topics as diverse as casket manufacturing, piano and organ manufacturing,

and York's industrial contribution to World War II. The 12,000-square-foot transportation wing showcases automobiles made in York, a Conestoga wagon, and a 1937 Aeronca K airplane.

The **Fire Museum** (757 W. Market St., 10am-4pm Sat. Apr.-Nov.) displays artifacts such as horse-drawn fire carriages, vintage fire trucks, and old-fashioned alarm systems.

USA Weightlifting Hall of Fame

If you've ever done bicep curls or bench presses, "York" probably rings a bell. The name is emblazoned on barbells, dumbbells, and other weightlifting equipment made by York Barbell, founded in York in 1932. Its manufacturing operations have shifted to other parts of the world, but the company still has administrative offices just north of the city. They're home to the **Weightlifting Hall of Fame** (3300 Board Rd., York, 717/767-6481, www.yorkbarbell.com, 10am-5pm Mon.-Sat., free admission), a must-stop for fans of strength sports. The Hall of Fame is part history museum and part homage to company founder and weightlifting legend Bob Hoffman. Raised near Pittsburgh, Hoffman was a sickly kid. In 1919, after serving in World War I, he moved to York and co-founded an oil burner company. Determined to build not just his business but also his body, Hoffman bought a barbell. By the late 1920s, the now-buff businessman was training other lifters and hiring them to work in his factory, which he eventually transformed from York Oil Burner into York Barbell. In 1946, when the United States won its first weightlifting world championship, four of the six teammates worked for York Barbell. Hoffman coached the U.S. Olympic team from 1948 to 1964, and York came to be known as "Muscletown USA."

A 7.5-foot bronze statue of Hoffman guards the entrance to the Hall of Fame. Exhibits trace the evolution of strength sports, highlighting legendary strongmen such as Joe "The Mighty Atom" Greenstein, whose feats

USA Weightlifting Hall of Fame

of strength included biting nails in half. Highlights of the collection include a seven-foot Travis dumbbell weighing more than 1,600 pounds. Its lifter and namesake, Warren Lincoln Travis, weighed just 180 pounds during his zenith in the early 1900s.

Steam Into History

On November 18, 1863, President Abraham Lincoln traveled by train from Washington DC to Gettysburg to deliver the speech that came to be known as the Gettysburg Address. One hundred and fifty years later, in 2013, the nonprofit **Steam Into History** (2 W. Main St., New Freedom, 717/942-2370, www.steamintohistory.com) began operating an excursion train on the rail line that carried him to York County's Hanover Junction, where the lanky leader stretched his legs before continuing on to Gettysburg. (Seventeen months later, the same line carried his funeral train through York County.) The train is pulled by a replica

the Steam Into History excursion train

of an 1860s steam locomotive. Many excursions feature reenactors, raconteurs, or musicians who help bring the Civil War era to life. Steam Into History offers round-trips from its headquarters in New Freedom to Glen Rock and Hanover Junction, which last one hour and two and a half hours, respectively. The train runs Tuesday-Sunday in the summer and select days in other seasons.

Haines Shoe House

Worth a stop if you're tootling along Route 30 or Route 462 (aka the Lincoln Highway) in western York County is the **Haines Shoe House** (197 Shoe House Rd., Hellam, 717/840-8339, www.shoehouse.us, 11am-5pm Wed.-Sun. June-Aug., 11am-5pm Sat.-Sun. Sept.-Oct., by appointment Nov.-May, tour $4.50, children 4-12 $3). Built in 1948, the shoe-shaped house was an advertising gimmick by "Shoe Wizard" Mahlon Haines, whose shoe empire grew to more than 40 stores in central Pennsylvania and northern Maryland. At first, the eccentric millionaire invited elderly couples to spend an expense-free weekend in the three-bedroom, two-bath shoe house. In 1950 he extended the invitation to honeymooning couples from any town with a Haines shoe store. After his death in 1962, the house became an ice cream parlor. Today the roadside oddity is a museum dedicated to Haines, who staged safaris on his nearby "Wizard Ranch" and used to stop smokers on the streets of York, offering them cash if they promised to quit.

The shoe motif is ubiquitous throughout the property. You'll find it on the wooden fence that surrounds the house and in the stained glass windows. There's even a shoe-shaped doghouse. Guided tours reveal other novelties, including a curved eating booth in the kitchen, located in the heel of the shoe house. Ice cream and other snacks are sold on-site, along with kitschy gifts like shoe house lamps with lighted windows.

Maize Quest Fun Park

In 1997, Hugh McPherson carved a maze into a cornfield in southern York County. It proved such a hit that in 2000, the Penn State graduate added a straw bale maze, a fence maze, and a maze of living bamboo. Year after year, **Maize Quest Fun Park** (2885 New Park Rd., New Park, 866/935-6738, www.mazefunpark. com) unveiled new attractions. Today it boasts more than 20, including an 80-foot-long tube slide, a stone labyrinth, a pumpkin patch, and peddle karts. The signature cornfield maze reflects a different theme each year. Past themes include "Ice Age Adventure," "Space Explorers," and "The Vikings!"

Maize Quest is open Friday-Sunday and holidays in the fall. Admission is $10 for adults, $8 for children 2-12. On Saturdays in winter and spring, it offers an indoor play area for kids ages 2-8. Admission to the "fun barn" is $7.50 for kids; there's no charge for adults.

ENTERTAINMENT AND EVENTS
Performing Arts

Downtown York's **Strand-Capitol Performing Arts Center** (50 N. George St., York, 717/846-1111, www.strandcapitol.org) plays host to touring musicians, dance companies, and comedians. The **York Symphony Orchestra** (717/812-0717, www.yorksymphony.org), which has performed without interruption since the Depression, can also be seen there. "There" is actually a five-building complex that includes two historic theaters. What's now known as the Capitol Theatre opened in 1906 as a dance hall and later became a movie house. The larger, grander Strand Theatre opened in 1925 primarily for vaudeville and silent movies. Both closed in the late 1970s as suburbia sucked the life out of downtown. But a movement to reopen them quickly took shape, and the Strand and Capitol reopened their doors in 1980 and 1981, respectively. At 500 seats, the Capitol is less than half the size of the Strand, but it boasts a restored 1927 Mighty Wurlitzer. The organ is put to use before classic film showings, which sometimes involve audience participation (e.g., singing along to *The Sound of*

Music or dressing like the title character in *The Big Lebowski*). Contemporary independent and foreign films are also shown at the Capitol.

Festivals and Events

Thousands of gleaming vintage cars of every description roll into York for **Street Rod Nationals East** (901/452-4030, www.nsra-usa.com, early June, admission charged), one of about a dozen annual events hosted by the National Street Rod Association. The street rods—vintage vehicles that have been modernized with features such as air-conditioning and cruise control—congregate on the grounds of the **York Expo Center** (334 Carlisle Ave., York, 717/848-2596, www.yorkexpo.com), where auto enthusiasts can get a close look and chat up the owners. Spectators line the streets of York for a parade of the candy-colored cars.

The Expo Center's signature event is the 10-day **York Fair** (717/848-2596, www.yorkfair.org, opens Friday after Labor Day, admission charged). The fair dates to 1765—11 years before the nation was founded—and bills itself as America's first and oldest. It was interrupted during the Civil War, when the fairgrounds served as a hospital for wounded soldiers, and in 1918 due to a deadly influenza outbreak. But the fair hasn't taken a hiatus since, growing larger and longer with each passing decade. It even remained open in the days following the 9/11 attacks, in celebration of American culture and spirit.

One of the most happening spots in York County, **Moon Dancer Vineyards & Winery** (1282 Klines Run Rd., Wrightsville, 717/252-9463, www.moondancerwinery.com, noon-5pm Wed.-Thurs., noon-10pm Fri., 11am-6pm Sat.-Sun.) hosts live music on Fridays, Saturdays, and Sundays year-round and a series of music festivals each summer. In the warmer months, visitors can mingle on the patio or picnic on the grounds of the French chateau-like winery overlooking the Susquehanna River. In the colder ones, they can sip hot mulled wine by a fire.

SPORTS AND RECREATION
Boating

The **lower section of Pennsylvania's Susquehanna River Water Trail** (717/252-0229, www.susquehannawatertrail.org), which forms the eastern boundary of York County, is beloved by paddlers and birders. It's home to the Conejohela Flats, a series of small islands and mud flats that attract scores of migratory shorebirds in spring and fall. You can get everything you need to hit the water at **Shank's Mare Outfitters** (2092 Long Level Rd., Wrightsville, 717/252-1616, www.shanksmare.com, open daily during boating season). Housed in an 1890s general store on the banks of the Susquehanna, the family-owned store sells and rents kayaks and stand-up paddleboards. On a calm day, it takes about 40 minutes to paddle from Shank's Mare to the Conejohela Flats. The store also offers guided paddle tours, kayaking and paddleboarding instruction, and guided hiking tours. The 193-mile **Mason-Dixon Trail** (www.masondixontrail.org) follows the west bank of the Susquehanna in York County, passing right by Shank's Mare.

Heritage Rail Trail

The 21-mile **Heritage Rail Trail** (717/840-7440, www.yorkcountyparks.org) stretches from York City to the Mason-Dixon line, where it connects to Maryland's 20-mile Northern Central Railroad Trail. It's open for hiking, bicycling, horseback riding, cross-country skiing, and snowshoeing. The parking lot for the York City trailhead is on Pershing Avenue near the Colonial Courthouse. Traversing the trail is part exercise, part history lesson. About six miles south of the reconstructed courthouse is the 370-foot Howard Tunnel, one of the oldest railroad tunnels in the country. The rail line adjacent to the Heritage Rail Trail was a vital link between Washington DC and points north in the 19th century. As such, it was a prime target for Confederate troops during the Civil War. After the Battle of Gettysburg in 1863,

President Lincoln traveled via these rails to deliver the Gettysburg Address, stretching his legs at York County's **Hanover Junction Station** (Rte. 616, Hanover Junction). The station at the midpoint of the Heritage Rail Trail has been restored to its 1863 appearance and houses a Civil War museum. There's another historic station near the southern end of the trail. The **New Freedom Station** (Front and Franklin Streets, New Freedom) has been restored to its 1940s appearance and houses a railroad museum. The museums are open on select days May-October. Check the York County Parks website for dates and times.

Four Springs Winery (50 Main St., Seven Valleys, 717/428-2610, www.fourspringswinerypa.com, 1pm-6pm Wed.-Fri., 11am-6pm Sat., 1pm-6pm Sun.) is also adjacent to the rail trail. It's not unusual to see spandex-clad cyclists in the tasting room.

Roundtop Mountain Resort

About midway between York and Harrisburg, **Roundtop Mountain Resort** (925 Roundtop Rd., Lewisberry, 717/432-9631, www.skiroundtop.com) offers skiing, snowboarding, and snow tubing in the colder months and activities like zip-lining

and bumper boating in the warmer ones. Homemade contraptions of cardboard, tape, and glue career down the tubing runs during Roundtop's annual **Cardboard Derby** in January. In summer, the tubing area becomes the site of an even zanier activity: rolling downhill in a giant plastic ball known as an OGO. Each OGO accommodates as many as three people.

ACCOMMODATIONS

Built during the Roaring Twenties, the 121-room ★ **Yorktowne Hotel** (48 E. Market St., York, 717/848-1111, www.yorktowne.com, $100-300) is resplendent with high ceilings, brass and crystal chandeliers, and wood paneling. Just as impressive is the service; some of the staff have worked at the downtown landmark for upwards of 20 years. The Yorktowne is conveniently located within walking distance of the Colonial Complex, the northern terminus of the Heritage Rail Trail, Central Market, and the Strand-Capitol Performing Arts Center.

York County has no shortage of excellent B&Bs. Among them: **Lady Linden Bed and Breakfast** (505 Linden Ave., York, 717/843-2929, www.ladylindenbedandbreakfast.

downtown York

com, $139), a meticulously restored 1887 Queen Anne Victorian with two guest suites. Breakfast is a four-course affair. **The Beechmont** (315 Broadway, Hanover, 717/632-3013, www.thebeechmont.com, $159-184) is an excellent choice in southern York County. Owner Kathryn White has received the Pennsylvania Tourism & Lodging Association's Innkeeper of the Year Award. The seven-room inn is convenient to historic Gettysburg. Now an oasis of calm, the house witnessed the Battle of Hanover, which delayed a Confederate cavalry's arrival at the more famous Battle of Gettysburg. White is a font of information about Hanover's role in the Civil War—and a whiz in the kitchen. Exquisite breakfasts are served by candlelight; homemade cookies or other treats are offered each evening.

FOOD

York's **Central Market** (34 W. Philadelphia St., York, 717/848-2243, www.centralmarketyork.com, 6am-2pm Tues., Thurs., and Sat.) is a hopping lunch spot. It's perfect for dining companions with different tastes, offering everything from soups and sandwiches to Caribbean and Malaysian dishes. On the downside, it's closed four days of the week.

Located across the street from Central Market, **White Rose Bar and Grill** (48 N. Beaver St., York, 717/848-5369, www.whiterosebarandgrill.com, 11am-10pm Sun.-Thurs., 11am-11pm Fri.-Sat., bar open until 2am Mon.-Sat. and midnight Sun., $5-35) dates to the 1930s. Extensive renovations in recent years have given it a thoroughly modern feel. The appetizer menu includes little neck clams, seared sushi-grade tuna, and plenty of deep-fried goodies, but nothing compares to the soft pretzel sticks topped with crab dip and melted cheese. Main dishes range from a simple BLT to seafood paella. Order from the "hot rock menu" and your seafood or steak will arrive at the table on heated volcanic stones, continuing to cook while you dig in.

York's most impressive martini list can be found at ★ **The Left Bank** (120 N. George St., York, 717/843-8010, www.leftbankyork. com, lunch Tues.-Fri., dinner Mon.-Sat., lunch $10-25, dinner $19-35), a chef-owned fine dining restaurant with a big-city feel. This is where Yorkers come on special occasions. Don't think "Philly cheesesteak" and "fancy" belong in the same sentence? You haven't tried chef David Albright's cheesesteak appetizer, made with beef tenderloin, bruschetta, and basil aioli. The seafood entrées are outstanding, as is the service. Don't hesitate to ask the waitstaff for wine recommendations.

If your visit to York County includes a visit to Moon Dancer Vineyards & Winery or Shank's Mare Outfitters, plan on dining at the nearby **John Wright Restaurant** (234 N. Front St., Wrightsville, 717/252-0416, www. johnwrightrestaurant.com, 11am-3pm Mon.-Tues., 11am-3pm and 4pm-9pm Wed.-Fri., 8am-9pm Sat., 11am-3pm Sun., lunch $7-14, dinner $12-27), which occupies a restored warehouse along the Susquehanna River. Heck, plan on dining there if you're anywhere within a 20-mile radius. The casual atmosphere, comfort foods, and killer views make it worth a drive. (You can also kayak to it.) Come for the Sunday brunch buffet ($16.95, children 3-12 $7.95) if you get the chance. In the warmer months, you can choose between the main restaurant and an outdoor dining area known as The Patio, which specializes in wood-fired pizzas. If you have to wait for a table, you can kill time in the **John Wright Store** (717/252-2519, www.johnwrightstore. com, 10am-4pm Mon.-Wed., 10am-8pm Thurs.-Fri., 9am-8pm Sat., 11am-3:30pm Sun.), which sells cast iron products, Vera Bradley accessories, Dansko shoes, and more.

INFORMATION

If you're arriving in York County via I-83 north, look for the state-run **welcome center** 2.5 miles north of the Pennsylvania-Maryland line. Personalized travel counseling is available 7am-7pm daily.

Visit the website of the **York County**

Convention & Visitors Bureau (717/852-9675, www.yorkpa.org) to request a free visitors guide or peruse a digital version. The CVB operates a visitors center in downtown York (149 W. Market St., 717/852-9675, 9:30am-4pm daily) and another at the Harley-Davidson plant (1425 Eden Rd., York, 717/852-6006, 9am-5pm daily).

GETTING THERE AND AROUND

York County shares its southern border with Maryland. Its county seat and largest municipality, York, is about 50 miles north of Baltimore and 25 miles south of Harrisburg via I-83. Route 30 provides east-west access to the city, which is about 30 miles from Gettysburg to its west and Lancaster to its east.

Harrisburg International Airport (MDT, 888/235-9442, www.flyhia.com), about half an hour's drive from York, is served by several major airlines. **Baltimore/Washington International Thurgood Marshall Airport** (BWI, 800/435-9294, www.bwiairport.com) is farther—about an hour from York assuming minimal traffic—but considerably larger.

Intercity bus service to York is available through **Greyhound** (53 E. North St., 800/231-2222, www.greyhound.com) and its interline partners. York County's public bus system is **Rabbittransit** (800/632-9063, www.rabbittransit.org).

Gettysburg and Vicinity

Few places in America have the name recognition of Gettysburg. There's hardly an eighth grader who hasn't heard of the town, which has fewer than 8,000 residents. It earned its place in the history books in 1863, when it was the setting for the Civil War's bloodiest battle and President Abraham Lincoln's most famous speech. The former took place July 1-3, with more than 165,000 soldiers converging on the crossroads town. Under the command of General George G. Meade, the Union army desperately and successfully defended its home territory from General Robert E. Lee's Confederate army. The war would continue for almost two years, but the Confederacy's hopes for independence effectively died on the Gettysburg Battlefield. The hellish battle's human toll was astronomical: 51,000 soldiers were dead, wounded, or missing. Interestingly, only one of Gettysburg's 2,400 citizens was killed during the biggest battle ever fought on this continent. The casualty was a young woman named Jennie Wade, and the bullet-riddled house in which she died is now a museum.

In the aftermath of the battle, the townspeople dedicated themselves to caring for the wounded and burying the dead. A group of prominent residents convinced the state to help fund the purchase of a portion of the battlefield to serve as a final resting place for the Union's defenders. Gettysburg attorney David Wills was appointed to coordinate the establishment of the Soldiers' National Cemetery, and he invited President Lincoln to deliver "a few appropriate remarks" at the dedication ceremony on November 19, 1863. The lanky commander-in-chief arrived by train the previous day and strolled down Carlisle Street to Wills's stately home on the town square. There, in a second-floor bedroom, he polished his talk. The National Park Service acquired the house in 2004 and opened it as a museum in 2009. Lincoln's two-minute Gettysburg Address—so succinct that a photographer on the scene failed to snap a picture—is regarded as the rhetorical zenith of his career and one of the greatest speeches in history.

The four-year Civil War was fought on many battlegrounds, but none is as hallowed as Gettysburg's. Established in 1895,

Gettysburg National Military Park was the first historic site owned by the U.S. government. As the only major Civil War battlefield in a northern state and an easy trip from population centers such as Philadelphia and Baltimore, it attracted scores of veterans and other visitors. The battlefield's popularity as a tourist destination bred commercial development in the 20th century. At one point there was even a casino on what is now park property. In recent years, preservationists have gotten the upper hand. Commercial establishments have been given the boot. Billboards have vanished. The National Park Service is even removing trees from parts of the battlefield, planting them in others, and reconstructing long-gone farm lanes and roads so that the landscape looks more like it did in 1863. Bottom line: There hasn't been a better time to visit Gettysburg in the last century. The picture of what transpired there is getting clearer and clearer.

PLANNING YOUR TIME

When to visit? That depends on your interests and tolerance for crowds. The Gettysburg area is busiest in early July, during the annual battle reenactment, which is held not on the battlefield but on private land. The town swarms with tourists and rifle-toting reenactors, and the weather tends toward hot and humid. Visitation tapers off as the summer draws to a close, then picks up in October, when paranormal enthusiasts flock to what they believe is one of the most haunted places in the country. Mid-November brings scores of Lincoln scholars and admirers. They discuss his life and legacy at an annual symposium before joining in a town-wide celebration of his famous address. Winter is the slow season, an ideal time for hushed contemplation of the carnage and courage that shaped this country. Some Gettysburg attractions are closed during the coldest months, but the battlefield is open daily year-round. Things pick up in April with the arrival of busload after busload of schoolchildren. By June, tourism is in full swing.

The battlefield is certainly the area's biggest draw, but there are more than a dozen other sights of interest to history buffs. Downtown Gettysburg is itself a historical attraction: About 60 percent of its buildings predate the battle. One of the most popular tourist stops isn't about history at all. It's a museum housing one man's collection of

living history in downtown Gettysburg

Gettysburg Guides

It's easy to explore Gettysburg on your own, but if you're hazy on Civil War history, a tour can make for a richer experience. Tour operators are a dime a dozen. Which one is right for you depends on your preferred mode of transport and whether you're keen on a live guide or satisfied with recorded narration. Many Gettysburg tours are led by members of the **Association of Licensed Battlefield Guides** (717/337-1709, www.gettysburgtourguides.org), who have spent years if not decades studying the Battle of Gettysburg. Licensure applicants first take a rigorous written exam; the highest scorers prove themselves further by passing an oral test. If you appreciate a lot of detail and ask a lot of questions, hire a licensed guide who will take the wheel of your car and show you around. Guides are available on a first-come, first-served basis at the **Gettysburg National Military Park Museum and Visitor Center** (1195 Baltimore Pike/Rte. 97, Gettysburg, 717/338-1243, reservations 717/334-2436, www.gettysburgfoundation.org, 8am-6pm daily Apr.-mid-Oct., 8am-5pm daily mid-Oct.-Mar.), but reservations are strongly recommended. A two-hour tour costs $65 per vehicle with 1-6 people, $90 per vehicle with 7-15. It's customary to tip your guide if you're satisfied. Bus tours with a licensed guide ($30, children 6-12 $18) also leave from the Museum and Visitor Center. Allow 2.5 hours for the bus tour.

Gettysburg Tours (778 Baltimore St., Gettysburg, 717/334-6296, www.gettysburgbattlefieldtours.com) offers two varieties of double-decker bus tours: one with a licensed guide ($30, children 6-12 $19) and another featuring recorded narration complete with cannon booms and rifle cracks ($26, children 6-12 $15). Both take about two hours. Gettysburg Tours operates several area attractions, including the Jennie Wade House and the Hall of Presidents & First Ladies. Combo packages are available.

You can feel like General Lee by touring the battlefield on horseback. **Artillery Ridge Campground** (610 Taneytown Rd., Gettysburg, 717/334-1288, www.artilleryridge.com), just across the street from the battlefield, offers one- and two-hour horseback tours ($50 and $80, respectively). Riding experience isn't necessary. Another option: gliding around the battlefield on a Segway.

elephants (man-made, not living). Another nonhistorical attraction, the Land of Little Horses (living, not man-made), scores big with kids.

★ GETTYSBURG NATIONAL MILITARY PARK

Expect to spend the better part of a day at **Gettysburg National Military Park** (717/334-1124, www.nps.gov/gett, 6am-10pm daily Apr.-Oct., 6am-7pm daily Nov.-Mar., free admission), site of the Civil War's biggest and bloodiest battle. The 6,000-acre park is not only one of the nation's most popular historical attractions but also one of the world's most extraordinary sculpture gardens. It's dotted with more than 1,300 monuments, markers, and memorials. They include equestrian bronzes of the battle's commanders, tributes to common soldiers, a statue of a civilian hero, and another of a priest who

gave absolution to Irish soldiers as they prepared for battle.

It's best to begin your visit at the **Museum and Visitor Center** (1195 Baltimore Pike/Rte. 97, Gettysburg, 717/338-1243, reservations 717/334-2436, www.gettysburgfoundation.org, 8am-6pm daily Apr.-mid-Oct., 8am-5pm daily mid-Oct.-Mar., admission to film/cyclorama/museum $12.50, seniors $11.50, children 6-12 $8.50), operated by the nonprofit Gettysburg Foundation. There you can orient yourself to the park and learn about the nightmarish clash of armies. Be sure to ask for a schedule of lectures, guided walks, and other special programs, which are especially frequent in the summer months. If you plan on touring the battlefield on your own, pick up the National Park Service map and guide (also available at www.nps.gov/gett). It outlines a 24-mile auto tour and briefly describes what transpired at each tour stop. For detailed descriptions of the three-day battle, you can

SegTours (22 Springs Ave., Gettysburg, 717/253-7987, www.segtours.com) offers a three-hour tour ($70) of the most famous battlefield sites and a two-hour tour ($50) to a lesser-known part of the battlefield, both with recorded narration. Live guides are available for an additional fee. Reservations are recommended for recorded tours and required for live guides. Tours depart on a regular schedule March-November. Off-season tours may be available by reservation.

Located in the bus parking lot at the Gettysburg National Military Park Museum and Visitor Center, **GettysBike** (1195 Baltimore Pike/Rte. 97, Gettysburg, 717/752-7752, www.gettysbike.com) offers bicycle tours of the battlefield and the town of Gettysburg. Led by licensed guides, the tours range from $51 to $71 per person. You can save $5 by bringing your own bike. GettysBike also offers bike rentals for those who want to explore on their own.

While most tours focus on the battlefield and the clashes of troops that culminated in a Union victory, the nonprofit **Main Street Gettysburg** (717/339-6161, www.mainstreetgettysburg.org) offers 90-minute walking tours of downtown that illumine the civilian experience. One need only to look at a map of Gettysburg National Military Park to realize that the town must have been deeply scarred. The battlefield enfolds the town—the last in America to be occupied by an invading army. Most walking tours ($16, seniors and children 6-18 $12) depart from the historic Gettysburg Hotel at 1 Lincoln Square.

Paranormal enthusiasts consider Gettysburg one of the most haunted places in the country. If you're not terribly squeamish, an evening ghost-themed tour may be for you. The original and most reputable operator is **Ghosts of Gettysburg** (271 Baltimore St., Gettysburg, 717/337-0445, www. ghostsofgettysburg.com, Mar.-Nov.) Its walking and bus tours, led by guides in period attire with candle lanterns in hand, are based on the books of historian, ghost hunter, and former National Park Service ranger Mark Nesbitt. Walking tours are $9.50-10 per person, free for children 7 and under. Bus tours are $18 per person, $16 for children 5-10, and off-limits to children under 5.

buy an audio tour CD in the museum bookstore or hire a federally licensed guide, who will get behind the wheel of your car and take you on a two-hour personalized tour ($65 per vehicle with 1-6 people). The highly knowledgeable guides are available on a first-come,

Gettysburg National Military Park

first-served basis as soon as the visitors center opens, but reservations are recommended. Bus tours with a licensed guide ($30, children 6-12 $18) are also offered.

The visitors center, which opened in 2008, is home to a colossal cyclorama depicting Pickett's Charge, a futile infantry assault ordered by Confederate General Robert E. Lee on the final day of battle. It's said that veterans wept at the sight of the 360-degree painting when it was unveiled in 1884. Measuring 42 feet high and 377 feet in circumference, the **Gettysburg Cyclorama** is the largest painting in the country. It's displayed with a diorama that gives the masterpiece a 3-D quality. A sound and light show amps up the drama. The cyclorama experience is preceded by a 22-minute film, *A New Birth of Freedom*, narrated by Morgan Freeman. Timed tickets are issued for the film and cyclorama. They include admission to the on-site **Gettysburg Museum of the American Civil War**, which explores the causes and consequences of the deadliest war in American history. Museum-only tickets are available.

The **Soldiers' National Cemetery**, where President Lincoln delivered his famous Gettysburg Address, is a short walk from the visitors center. It's open from dawn to sunset and closed to vehicular traffic. Walking tour brochures are available at the visitors center and online at www.nps.gov/gett. Work on the cemetery began soon after the bloodshed ended. Thousands of Union and Confederate dead had been hastily buried on or near the battlefield, many of them in shallow graves. Heavy rains would expose decaying bodies, a grisly sight that helped convince Pennsylvania governor Andrew Curtin to appropriate state funds for the cemetery project. About 3,500 Union soldiers were interred there. The Confederate dead remained in scattered graves until the 1870s, when they were relocated to cemeteries in the south. Today the Soldiers' National Cemetery is the final resting place for veterans from all of America's wars through Vietnam. It's the setting for several annual events, including a Memorial Day service and a commemoration of the Gettysburg Address held each November.

OTHER SIGHTS
Gettysburg Seminary Ridge Museum

The **Seminary Ridge Museum** (111 Seminary Ridge, Gettysburg, 717/339-1300, www.seminaryridgemuseum.org, 10am-5pm Fri.-Mon., admission $9, seniors and children

the Gettysburg Cyclorama

6-12 $7) opened July 1, 2013, exactly 150 years after the Battle of Gettysburg erupted. That first day of battle is one of the museum's main focuses. Built in 1832 for the Lutheran Theological Seminary at Gettysburg, the museum building was used as a field hospital during the 1863 battle. Appropriately enough, the new museum also places special emphasis on Civil War medicine and the moral and spiritual debates of that tumultuous era. It features four floors of exhibits, large-scale reproductions of 10 commissioned paintings by renowned historical artist Dale Gallon, interactive stations for children, and an outdoor interpretive trail. The building's cupola, which was used by Union General John Buford to survey the battlefield, is accessible by guided tour. You must be at least 13 years old and able to climb stairs to take the cupola tour ($29, seniors $27, includes museum admission).

Eisenhower National Historic Site

Located adjacent to the Gettysburg Battlefield, **Eisenhower National Historic Site** (717/338-9114, www.nps.gov/eise, admission $7.50, children 6-12 $5) preserves the one-time home and farm of President Dwight D. Eisenhower. The Texas-born Army general and 34th president first visited Gettysburg as a cadet at the U.S. Military Academy at West Point and returned during World War I to run a training camp. After commanding the Allied forces during the Second World War, "Ike" came to Gettysburg with his wife, Mamie, in search of a retirement home. The house has changed little since then. Furnishings include a coffee table given to the Eisenhowers by the first lady of South Korea, a rug from the shah of Iran, and a desk fashioned from old floorboards removed from the White House during a 1948 renovation. Visitors can also explore the grounds, which include a putting green, rose gardens, and a garage that still houses the Eisenhowers' jeep, golf carts, and station wagon. Due to limited on-site parking and space in the home, visitors must arrive by shuttle bus from the Museum and Visitor Center at Gettysburg National Military Park (1195 Baltimore Pike/Rte. 97, Gettysburg, 717-338-1243, reservations 717/334-2436, www.gettysburgfoundation.org). Shuttles depart every hour or half hour 9am-4pm during most times of the year.

Shriver and Jennie Wade Houses

These two house museums explore the civilian

Eisenhower National Historic Site

experience during the Civil War. Both feature tour guides in period attire.

The **Shriver House Museum** (309 Baltimore St., Gettysburg, 717/337-2800, www.shriverhouse.org, open daily Apr.-mid-Nov., call or check website for off-season hours, admission $8.50, seniors $8.25, children under 13 $6.35) tells the story of George Washington Shriver and his family. In 1860, Shriver paid $290 for what was then considered a double lot on the edge of town. He built a home for his family, opening a saloon in the cellar and a 10-pin bowling alley in an adjacent building. When the Civil War erupted in 1861, Shriver answered President Lincoln's call for troops. He was still away when the war came to Gettysburg in July 1863. While his wife and two young daughters hunkered down at her parents' farm about three miles away, Confederate soldiers occupied their home. Today visitors learn about life during the Civil War as they tour all four floors of the house, including the attic used by Confederate sharpshooters. Three live Civil War bullets and period medical supplies were discovered under floorboards when the house was under restoration in 1996. They're among the artifacts displayed in the museum shop next door.

The nearby **Jennie Wade House** (548 Baltimore St., Gettysburg, 717/334-4100, www.gettysburgbattlefieldtours.com, hours vary by season, admission $7.75, children 6-12 $4) is a shrine to the only civilian casualty of the Battle of Gettysburg. Jennie Wade was baking bread for Union soldiers when bullets ripped through the door of the house, taking her life. She was 20 years old and engaged to a childhood friend who'd been mustered into the service two years earlier. He died just nine days later of wounds sustained in a Virginia battle, never knowing of his sweetheart's fate.

General Lee's Headquarters Museum

On the first day of the Battle of Gettysburg, Confederate General Robert E. Lee established his personal headquarters in a stone house at the center and rear of his battle lines. There, he and his commanders pondered the problems of the great battle, which ended in a victory for the Union. Fifty-nine years after Lee escaped south, the house was opened to the public as a museum named for him. **General Lee's Headquarters Museum** (401 Buford Ave., Gettysburg, 717/334-3141, www.civilwar-headquarters.com, 9am-5pm mid-Mar.-Nov., extended summer hours, free admission) is one of the oldest museums in Gettysburg and unique in its focus on the Confederate cause. It's also unique in that visitors can spend a night upstairs. The **Quality Inn at General Lee's Headquarters** (717/334-3141, www.thegettysburgaddress.com, $65-250) has hosted such bigwigs as General George Patton and President Dwight Eisenhower as well as the last surviving Confederate widow.

Wax Museums

The little town of Gettysburg is home to not one but two wax museums. More than 300 life-size wax figures depict events of the nation's deadliest war at the **American Civil War Wax Museum** (297 Steinwehr Ave., Gettysburg, 717/334-6245, www.gettysburgmuseum.com, 9am-5pm daily Mar.-Dec., extended spring and summer hours, open weekends and holidays Jan.-Feb., admission $6.95, children 6-17 $3.95). Visitors learn about the economic, social, and political causes of the war, the assassination of President Abraham Lincoln, and everything in between. The sounds of bullets and battle cries echo in the Battle Auditorium, home to a life-size diorama of the Battle of Gettysburg. The **Gettysburg Gift Center,** located in the lobby of the museum, is one of the largest and best gift shops in town.

A stone's throw from the main entrance to Soldiers' National Cemetery, the **Hall of Presidents & First Ladies** (789 Baltimore St., Gettysburg, 717/334-5717, www.gettysburgbattlefieldtours.com, hours vary by season, admission $7.50, children 6-12 $3.50) features wax figures of every American president. Extra attention is paid to 34th President Dwight D. Eisenhower, who bought a home in Gettysburg before winning the presidency and lived out his days there. The museum also has a collection of doll-size first ladies in their inaugural gowns.

Land of Little Horses Farm Park

Admission isn't cheap, but the **Land of Little Horses** (125 Glenwood Dr., Gettysburg, 717/334-7259, www.landoflittlehorses.com, 10am-5pm Mon.-Sat. and noon-5pm Sun. May-late Aug., Sat.-Sun. only through Oct., admission $15.95, children 6-11 $13.95, children 2-5 $11.95) is a hit with little 'uns. Just a few miles west of downtown Gettysburg, the "performing animal theme park" is home to not only miniature horses but also goats, sheep, donkeys, emus, and other critters. Animal performances are held daily in the summer and on weekends in spring and fall. The park also offers pony rides and wagon rides at $5 a pop. (Alas, if you're over 70 pounds, no pony ride for you.)

Mister Ed's Elephant Museum & Candy Emporium

Ed Gotwalt's passion for all things pachyderm started on his wedding day more than 40 years ago, when he received an elephant knickknack as a good luck charm. By 1983 his elephant collection had grown so large that he opened a museum to showcase it. Miss Ellie Phant, a life-size talking elephant with animated eyes and ears, greets visitors at **Mister Ed's Elephant Museum** (6019 Chambersburg Rd., Orrtanna, 717/352-3792, www.mistereds. com, 10am-6pm Sun.-Thurs., 10am-8pm Fri.-Sat., free admission), located on Route 30 about 12 miles west of Gettysburg. It doesn't cost a cent to see Gotwalt's collection, which has ballooned to more than 12,000 elephants. After a 2010 fire claimed roughly 2,000 elephants, thousands more arrived from donors around the world. There are stone elephants, wood elephants, metal elephants, and plush elephants. There's an elephant potty chair and an elephant hair dryer. There are even elephant-embroidered pillowcases that once belonged to Cher.

Elephants aren't the only draw. The **Candy Emporium** features fresh roasted peanuts, more than 70 flavors of fudge, and old-time candy like wax bottles and Pez.

Appalachian Trail Museum

After 12 years in the making, the **Appalachian Trail Museum** (1120 Pine Grove Rd., Gardners, 717/486-8126, www. atmuseum.org, open spring-fall, hours vary by season, free admission) opened in 2010. Housed in a former gristmill in Pine Grove Furnace State Park, the museum pays tribute to pioneer hikers such as Earl Shaffer, the first person to thru-hike the trail, and "Grandma" Gatewood, who was 67 when she became the first female to complete the journey alone. There's even an exhibit on Ziggy, the first feline to conquer the Georgia-to-Maine trail. (To be fair, the cat spent most of the journey riding on the backpack of hiker Jim "the Geek" Adams, but he contributed much in the way of mice patrol at trail shelters.) Highlights of the collection include a trail shelter that Shaffer, a native of nearby York County, built about a decade after his 1948 history-making hike. The shelter was painstakingly dismantled at its original site and reassembled in the museum.

Visitors stand a good chance of rubbing shoulders with modern-day thru-hikers because the museum is just a few hundred yards off the Appalachian Trail. The midpoint of the 2,180-mile footpath is just south of **Pine Grove Furnace State Park** (1100 Pine Grove Rd., Gardners, 717/486-7174, www.visitpa-parks.com), and tradition dictates that thru-hikers stop at the park's general store to face a test of mettle known as the "half-gallon challenge." Those who succeed, i.e., eat half a gallon of ice cream in one sitting, are rewarded with a commemorative wooden spoon. Word has it that chunky flavors are harder to finish.

The state park is named for an ironworks founded in 1764, and the charcoal iron furnace that operated until 1895 is still standing. A mansion built in 1829 for the ironmaster's family now serves as a hostel and event venue. The 696-acre park also features a campground and two small lakes with beaches and a boat rental. Pine Grove allows overnight parking for anyone who wants to hit the A.T., but registration at the park office is required.

National Apple Museum

Adams County, of which Gettysburg is the county seat, is one of the largest apple producers in the country and the heart of Pennsylvania's fruit belt. It's home to grower-owned applesauce maker Musselman's, a Mott's plant, and the **National Apple Museum** (154 W. Hanover St., Biglerville, 717/677-4556, www.nationalapplemuseum. com, 10am-4pm Sat. and 1pm-4pm Sun. May-Oct., admission $3, seniors $2, children 6-16 $1.50). Miles and miles of orchards make for scenic drives, especially when the trees are in bloom. Visit the **Gettysburg Wine & Fruit Trail** website (www.gettysburgwineandfruittrail.com) for a map highlighting orchards, farm markets, and other agritourism attractions.

ENTERTAINMENT AND EVENTS
Performing Arts

The **Majestic Theater** (25 Carlisle St., Gettysburg, 717/337-8200, www.gettysburgmajestic.org) was the largest vaudeville and silent movie theater in south-central Pennsylvania when it opened in 1925. President Dwight D. Eisenhower and First Lady Mamie Eisenhower attended performances in the 1950s, often with world leaders in tow. In 1993 the Majestic hosted the world premiere of *Gettysburg*, one of the longest films ever released by a Hollywood studio. Today it hosts live performances by the likes of the Moscow Circus, the Temptations, and pianist Jim Brickman. Two cinemas with stadium seating were added as part of a $16 million renovation in recent years. The Majestic screens indie and critically acclaimed films seven days a week.

Festivals and Events

The Gettysburg area is apple country. It's home to apple orchards, applesauce makers, and even an apple museum. It also boasts two annual apple-themed festivals. Both feature orchard tours, pony rides, antique cars, arts and crafts vendors, live entertainment, and

an event at the National Apple Harvest Festival

more. Held the first full weekend in May, when apple trees are in bloom, the **Apple Blossom Festival** (717/677-7444, www.appleblossomfestival.info, admission $5, children under 12 free) also includes a "PA Apple Queen" contest. The reigning Apple Queen makes appearances at the **National Apple Harvest Festival** (717/677-9413, www.appleharvest. com, first two full weekends in Oct., admission $9, seniors $8, children under 12 free), the region's biggest to-do. Both festivals are held at the South Mountain Fair Grounds, 10 miles northwest of Gettysburg on Route 234.

Thousands of reenactors take part in the annual **Gettysburg Civil War Battle Reenactment** (information 717/334-6274, tickets 800/514-3849, www.gettysburggreenactment.com, early July, admission charged), firing period weapons and feigning death on farm fields just a few miles from the original battlefield. Several clashes are staged over three days. Spectators can stroll through the soldiers' camps, listen to live Civil War music and period speakers, watch period demonstrations, and shop for period wares. Arrive early to claim a spot near the front of battle viewing areas. It's a good idea to bring folding chairs, binoculars, and sunscreen. Limited bleacher seating is available but usually sells out before the event.

A host of events commemorate President Abraham Lincoln's Gettysburg Address, delivered at the dedication of the Soldiers' National Cemetery less than five months after the Battle of Gettysburg. Held on the speech's anniversary, **Dedication Day** (717/338-1243, www.gettysburgfoundation.org, Nov. 19) begins with a wreath-laying ceremony at the cemetery. Nationally renowned Lincoln actor Jim Getty recites the short speech after an oration by a person of note. Past speakers have included actor Richard Dreyfuss, newsman Tom Brokaw, astronaut Neil Armstrong, and Chief Justice William Rehnquist. Held within a few days of Dedication Day, **Remembrance Day** (717/232-7000, www.suvcw.org) features a parade of Civil War reenactors—from drummer boys to generals on horseback—that

winds through Gettysburg and ends at the National Military Park. As the day draws to a close, a luminary candle is placed on each Civil War grave in the Soldiers' National Cemetery. The cost to sponsor a candle for the **Remembrance Illumination** (717/339-2148, www.friendsofgettysburg.org) is, appropriately enough, $18.63.

SHOPPING
Downtown Gettysburg
You won't find the Gap or a Starbucks in downtown Gettysburg. Its shops are of the independent variety, and many offer things you'd be hard-pressed to find in a big city: Civil War collectibles, military artifacts from the American Revolutionary War and onward, and anything a reenactor could want, from candle lanterns to cavalry swords. Dale Gallon, one of the nation's premier historical artists, has an eponymous gallery in town: the **Gallon Historical Art Gallery** (9 Steinwehr Ave., 717/334-8666, www.gallon.com, call for hours).

Greater Gettysburg
Pennsylvania's sales tax exemption on clothing lures many a Marylander to the **Outlet Shoppes at Gettysburg** (1863 Gettysburg Village Dr., Gettysburg, 717/337-9705, www. theoutletshoppesatgettysburg.com, 10am-9pm Mon.-Sat., 10am-6pm Sun.) at Route 15 and Baltimore Street (Route 97). Stores include Jones New York, Old Navy, Tommy Hilfiger, Naturalizer, and Coach. There's a 10-screen movie theater (717/338-0101) and hotel on-site.

The quiet, tree-lined borough of **New Oxford,** 10 miles east of Gettysburg on Route 30, is an antiquing mecca with more than 500 dealers. A partial list can be found at www. newoxfordantiques.com, website of the New Oxford Antique Dealers Association.

ACCOMMODATIONS
Gettysburg has loads of lodging properties, many of which have a story to tell. There are B&Bs scarred by bullets and rooms once

occupied by generals. You can unwind in a place that once crawled with wounded soldiers. If you visit when the town is crawling with tourists, expect two- or three-night minimums at many properties. Rates are at their lowest from December through March.

Under $100

Camping is a popular and inexpensive way to stay near the battlefield during the high season. Gettysburg has half a dozen campgrounds. If your idea of camping is quietly communing with nature, you may be in for a shock. These campgrounds are fairly bustling places. Some have cottages so luxurious they make hotel rooms look rustic, and all offer a host of modern amenities. **Drummer Boy Camping Resort** (1300 Hanover St., Gettysburg, 800/293-2808, www.drummerboycampresort.com, tent site $38-57, hookup site $44-80, cabin or cottage $65-360, weekly rates available) has, in addition to more than 400 campsites and about 50 cabins and cottages, two heated pools, a 250-foot waterslide, a mini golf course, a game room, basketball and volleyball courts, and a fishing pond. Add to that a full schedule of activities and it's a wonder that campers ever leave the 95-acre resort. Drummer Boy is a few minutes east of downtown on Route 116.

A few minutes west of downtown on Route 116 is the 260-site **Gettysburg Campground** (2030 Fairfield Rd./Rte. 116 W., Gettysburg, 717/334-3304, www.gettysburgcampground.com, tent site $33-46, hookup site $37-66, cabin or cottage $65-165, weekly rates available). It too has amenities up the wazoo. Try to snag a campsite along Marsh Creek.

$100-200

Gettysburg's most iconic hotel, the ★ **Best Western Gettysburg Hotel** (1 Lincoln Square, Gettysburg, 717/337-2000, www.hotelgettysburg.com, peak season $138-390, winter $100-250), is said to have a friendly ghost. You may or may not encounter the Civil War nurse named Rachel during your stay. You'll definitely encounter friendly staff. The hotel in the center of town, just steps from the house where President Lincoln polished his Gettysburg Address, is steeped in history. Its story begins in 1797, when a tavern opened its doors on the site. It withstood the bloody and pivotal battle of 1863 but was replaced in the 1890s by the current structure, which was christened the Hotel Gettysburg. In 1955 the hotel served as President Eisenhower's national operations center while he recuperated from a heart attack at his Gettysburg home. Eisenhower and his wife were the hotel's last guests before it closed its doors in 1964, rendered unprofitable by changes in travel habits. Ravaged by fire in 1983, the building was painstakingly restored and opened as a Best Western in 1991, grand as it ever was. The hotel has 119 guest accommodations, almost half of which are suites; a rooftop swimming pool; and a fine dining restaurant. Check the website for a list of packages that bundle accommodations with activities such as skiing and theater-going.

Also historic but considerably smaller, the **James Gettys Hotel** (27 Chambersburg St., Gettysburg, 717/337-1334, www.jamesgettyshotel.com, $145-250) is half a block from the town square. Named for the founder of Gettysburg, it dates to 1804 and looks much as it did in the 1920s. Like the Gettysburg Hotel, it closed in the 1960s and reopened as an emulation of its former self in the 1990s. The James Gettys has a dozen suites, each with a bedroom, sitting room, kitchenette, and private bath. A complimentary continental breakfast is delivered to guests daily. Housekeeping has been known to leave behind dark chocolates in the shape of the hotel.

With more than 300 guest rooms and suites, the **Eisenhower Hotel** (2634 Emmitsburg Rd., Gettysburg, 717/334-8121, www.eisenhower.com, $119-149) is the largest hotel in the area. Amenities include an indoor pool and whirlpool tub, a fitness room, dry saunas, a casual eatery, and a business center. A fun park on the hotel grounds features two go-kart tracks, 36 holes of miniature golf, a 14-acre fishing lake, and batting cages. Downtown Gettysburg is five miles to the north, and the battlefield is even closer.

B&B options in downtown Gettysburg include the impeccable ★ **Brickhouse Inn Bed & Breakfast** (452 Baltimore St., Gettysburg, 717/338-9337, www.brickhouse-inn.com, $119-189). The older of its two buildings dates to the 1830s and was occupied by Confederate sharpshooters during the Battle of Gettysburg. Its south wall still bears the scars of Union bullets. The main house is an 1898 Victorian with original wood floors and chestnut trim. Between them they have 14 guest rooms and suites, each named for a state represented in the bloody battle. Breakfast always includes a hot entrée and the B&B's signature shoofly pie. Proprietors Tessa Bardo and Brian Duncan will give you the shirts off their backs but not the secret family recipe.

A few miles south of town is a countryside oasis, the **Lightner Farmhouse Bed & Breakfast** (2350 Baltimore Pike, Gettysburg, 717/337-9508, www.lightnerfarmhouse.com, $139-195). Built shortly before the Battle of Gettysburg, the Federal-style farmhouse was used as a hospital for three weeks after the bloodshed. Nothing gory about the place today. Innkeepers Dennis and Eileen Hoover aim to provide "outrageous service," whether preparing breakfast or arranging a crash course in paranormal investigation. The B&B has five en suite rooms, a suite that sleeps up to four, and a two-floor cottage with a private wraparound deck. Quilt designs inspired the decor. Nature trails wind through the 19-acre property.

Built circa 1797, the **Cashtown Inn** (1325 Old Rte. 30, Cashtown, 717/334-9722, www.cashtowninn.com, $145-200) was the first stagecoach stop west of Gettysburg. It owes its name to its original innkeeper, who accepted only cash. These days, credit cards are welcome at the inn, which is known as much for its cuisine as its cozy accommodations. Its four rooms and three suites are named for Confederate generals, some of whom made their headquarters there during the summer of 1863. More recent (and welcome) guests have included actor Sam Elliott, who bunked there while filming the 1993 movie *Gettysburg,* and paranormal investigator Jason Hawes, who featured the Cashtown in an episode of the Syfy series *Ghost Hunters.* Room rates include breakfast.

FOOD

Gettysburg is no dining mecca, but it offers a rare opportunity for culinary time travel. A number of restaurants specialize in period fare. Best of the bunch: the **Dobbin House Tavern** (89 Steinwehr Ave., Gettysburg, 717/334-2100, www.dobbinhouse.com), offering colonial and continental cuisine in Gettysburg's oldest building. The Dobbin House was built in 1776—the same year the American colonies declared their independence from Great Britain—as a home for an Irish-born minister and his large brood. It served as a station on the Underground Railroad in the mid-1800s and as a hospital

the Dobbin House Tavern

in the immediate aftermath of the Battle of Gettysburg. Great pains have been taken to restore the house-turned-restaurant to its 18th-century appearance. Many of the antique furnishings match descriptions in the inventory of the minister's estate. The china and flatware match fragments unearthed during an excavation of the cellar. For casual dining, head to the basement Springhouse Tavern (open daily from 11:30am, $8-25). With three natural springs and two fireplaces, it's a cozy and romantic spot (that can be clammy in winter and humid in summer). Specials include spit-roasted chicken, chargrilled strip steak, and barbecued ribs, all served with a hearth-baked roll. Fine dining is available in six candlelit rooms known as the Alexander Dobbin Dining Rooms (open daily from 5pm, $17-37). The "bedroom" features a table beneath a lace bed canopy. Servers in period attire help satisfy the craving for history that brings most visitors to Gettysburg. Reservations are accepted for the dining rooms but not the tavern, where you can expect a considerable wait on summer weekends.

The **Farnsworth House Inn** (401 Baltimore St., Gettysburg, 717/334-8838, www.farnsworthhouseinn.com, dining rooms 5pm-9pm daily, call for winter hours, $17-26)

is another popular destination for period dining complete with costumed servers. Game pie, the house specialty, is a stew of turkey, pheasant, and duck topped with a golden egg crust. Built in the early 1800s, the house sheltered Confederate sharpshooters during the Battle of Gettysburg. It's believed that one of them accidentally shot Jennie Wade, the only civilian killed during the three-day struggle. Oil paintings of the commanding officers at Gettysburg and photos by famed Civil War photographer Mathew Brady decorate the bullet-scarred house, which has been restored to its 1863 appearance. Its tavern (11:30am-10pm daily, call for winter hours, $8-18), popular with reenactors, offers hot and cold sandwiches, pork and sauerkraut, meatloaf, and more. Garden dining is available in the warmer months.

Eight miles west of Gettysburg on Route 116, the **Fairfield Inn** (15 W. Main St., Gettysburg, 717/642-5410, www.thefairfield-inn.com, lunch 11am-2pm Fri.-Sat., brunch 11am-2pm Sun., dinner 5pm-7:45pm Tues.-Sat., lunch $6-12, dinner $19-32) has hosted such VIPs as Thaddeus Stevens and President Dwight D. Eisenhower since opening in 1757. The day after the Battle of Gettysburg, as the weary Confederate army retreated west

the Fairfield Inn

through Fairfield, the inn hosted their generals. Today's guests can sup on hearty ham and bean soup and chicken and biscuits, just like General Robert E. Lee, or choose from dishes like Tuscan penne, fried haddock, and roasted half duck with balsamic fig reduction.

If you're not into period dining, you're not out of luck. The Gettysburg area has some recommendable restaurants that go a different route. **Gettysburg Eddie's** (217 Steinwehr Ave., Gettysburg, 717/334-1100, www.gettysburgeddies.com, 11am-10pm Mon.-Thurs., 11am-10:30pm Fri.-Sat., 11am-9pm Sun., bar open until 11pm Mon.-Thurs., midnight Fri.-Sat., and 10pm Sun., call for winter hours, $6-27), across the street from Soldiers' National Cemetery, is a casual, welcoming spot with a stamp of approval from the sustainability-promoting Green Restaurant Association. Named for Baseball Hall of Fame pitcher Eddie Plank, born in 1875 on a farm north of Gettysburg, the restaurant has an expansive menu that includes foot-long franks, steaks, sizzling fajitas, and pasta dishes. The housemade peanut butter pie is a home run. Big LCD TVs and a full-service bar make Eddie's a popular place to watch college and pro sports.

Herr Tavern & Publick House (900 Chambersburg Rd., Gettysburg, 717/334-4332, www.herrtavern.com, lunch 11am-3pm Wed.-Sat., dinner 5pm-9pm daily, lunch $7-15, dinner $24-34) is an excellent choice for fine dining. Servers are happy to talk guests through the creative menu, which changes frequently, and extensive wine list, a winner of *Wine Enthusiast Magazine's* Unique Distinction Award. Built in 1815, the tavern was turned into a Confederate hospital during the 1863 clash of armies. It's said that amputated limbs were thrown out of a window into a waiting wagon. Given the gruesomeness of what went down, it's no wonder the staff have some ghost stories to share. Herr Tavern is just west of downtown Gettysburg on Route 30. A few miles farther west is another historic and

reportedly haunted dining destination. The ★ **Cashtown Inn** (1325 Old Rte. 30, Cashtown, 717/334-9722, www.cashtowninn.com, lunch 11:30am-2pm and dinner from 5pm Tues.-Sat., lunch $6-11, dinner $20-33) was also overrun by Confederates during the battle. The general who assumed command of the defeated army's retreat made it his headquarters. Its current owners have resisted the temptation to lure history-hungry tourists with period fare, offering New American cuisine instead. They rely on local farmers and producers for everything from eggs and apples to wine and beer.

INFORMATION

Destination Gettysburg (717/334-6274, www.destinationgettysburg.com) is a good source of information about the area. Visit its website to request a free copy of its official visitors guide or peruse a digital version. Destination Gettysburg has information desks in the Museum and Visitor Center at Gettysburg National Military Park (1195 Baltimore Pike/Rte. 97, Gettysburg, open daily) and in the historic train station in downtown Gettysburg (35 Carlisle St., open daily Mar.-Nov., closed Tues.-Wed. Dec.-Feb.).

GETTING THERE

Gettysburg is in the center of Adams County, which hugs the Pennsylvania-Maryland line just west of York County. It's about 45 miles southwest of **Harrisburg International Airport** (MDT, 888/235-9442, www.flyhia.com) via I-76 west and Route 15 south and 60 miles northwest of the larger **Baltimore/Washington International Thurgood Marshall Airport** (BWI, 800/435-9294, www.bwiairport.com). Private aircraft can fly into **Gettysburg Regional Airport** (888/235-9442, www.flyhia.com) just west of town.

There's no passenger train or commercial bus service to Gettysburg. It's very much a driving destination.

Photo Credits

MAP SYMBOLS

▦▦▦ Expressway	★	Highlight	✗	Airfield	⌁	Golf Course
▦▦▦ Primary Road	○	City/Town	✗	Airport	🅿	Parking Area
▦▦▦ Secondary Road	◉	State Capital	▲	Mountain	⬠	Archaeological Site
◦◦◦◦ Unpaved Road	◉	National Capital	✛	Unique Natural Feature	⬥	Church
------ Trail	★	Point of Interest			▯	Gas Station
⋯⋯⋯ Ferry	•	Accommodation	⋎	Waterfall	◌	Glacier
◦—◦— Railroad	▼	Restaurant/Bar	▲	Park	▨	Mangrove
▦▦▦ Pedestrian Walkway	▪	Other Location	▣	Trailhead	▨	Reef
▥▥▥ Stairs	Λ	Campground	⛷	Skiing Area	▨	Swamp

CONVERSION TABLES

°C = (°F - 32) / 1.8
°F = (°C x 1.8) + 32
1 inch = 2.54 centimeters (cm)
1 foot = 0.304 meters (m)
1 yard = 0.914 meters
1 mile = 1.6093 kilometers (km)
1 km = 0.6214 miles
1 fathom = 1.8288 m
1 chain = 20.1168 m
1 furlong = 201.168 m
1 acre = 0.4047 hectares
1 sq km = 100 hectares
1 sq mile = 2.59 square km
1 ounce = 28.35 grams
1 pound = 0.4536 kilograms
1 short ton = 0.90718 metric ton
1 short ton = 2,000 pounds
1 long ton = 1.016 metric tons
1 long ton = 2,240 pounds
1 metric ton = 1,000 kilograms
1 quart = 0.94635 liters
1 US gallon = 3.7854 liters
1 Imperial gallon = 4.5459 liters
1 nautical mile = 1.852 km

°FAHRENHEIT °CELSIUS

230 — 110
220 —
210 — 100 WATER BOILS
200 —
190 — 90
180 — 80
170 —
160 — 70
150 —
140 — 60
130 —
120 — 50
110 —
100 — 40
90 —
80 — 30
70 — 20
60 —
50 — 10
40 —
30 — 0 WATER FREEZES
20 —
10 — -10
0 —
-10 — -20
-20 — -30
-30 —
-40 — -40

0   1   2   3   4
INCH

0 1 2 3 4 5 6 7 8 9 10
CM

MOON SPOTLIGHT PENNSYLVANIA DUTCH COUNTRY

Avalon Travel
a member of the Perseus Books Group
1700 Fourth Street
Berkeley, CA 94710, USA
www.moon.com

Editor: Nikki Ioakimedes
Contributor: Dan Eldridge
Series Manager: Kathryn Ettinger
Copy Editor: Alissa Cyphers
Graphics Coordinator: Elizabeth Jang
Production Coordinator: Elizabeth Jang
Cover Design: Faceout Studios, Charles Brock
Moon Logo: Tim McGrath
Map Editor: Kat Bennett
Cartographer: Stephanie Poulain

ISBN-13: 978-1-61238-790-1

ABOUT THE AUTHOR

Anna Dubrovsky

Anna Dubrovsky was born in St. Petersburg, Russia. She has lived in more than a dozen cities on three continents and has explored countless others, yet Pennsylvania keeps pulling her back.

Anna first set foot in the Keystone State when her seventh-grade class ventured from Cleveland to Philadelphia, belting Whitney Houston ballads all the way. Her family relocated to Pittsburgh a few years later; Anna's first driver's license was a Pennsylvania one. After beginning college at Northwestern University, she returned to Pennsylvania for reporting internships at *The Pittsburgh Post-Gazette* and *The Morning Call* of Allentown, where she covered the Great Allentown Fair from the perspective of a sheep. Upon graduating, she wrote about state government and politics for the *York Daily Record*.

After stints as a political journalist in New York City, a financial reporter in New Jersey and Los Angeles, and a student of yoga in India, Anna followed her heart back to Pennsylvania, where she became a wife, mother, and Moon author. You can find her online at www.anywherebutacubicle.com.